OECD Budget Transparency Toolkit

PRACTICAL STEPS FOR SUPPORTING OPENNESS, INTEGRITY AND ACCOUNTABILITY IN PUBLIC FINANCIAL MANAGEMENT

Developed by the OECD with the participation of the Global Initiative for Fiscal Transparency (GIFT) Network

This work is published under the responsibility of the Secretary-General of the OECD. The opinions expressed and arguments employed herein do not necessarily reflect the official views of OECD member countries.

This document, as well as any data and any map included herein, are without prejudice to the status of or sovereignty over any territory, to the delimitation of international frontiers and boundaries and to the name of any territory, city or area.

Please cite this publication as:
OECD (2017), *OECD Budget Transparency Toolkit: Practical Steps for Supporting Openness, Integrity and Accountability in Public Financial Management*, OECD Publishing, Paris.
http://dx.doi.org/10.1787/9789264282070-en

ISBN 978-92-64-28206-3 (print)
ISBN 978-92-64-28207-0 (PDF)

Photo credits: Cover © Poeli Bojorquez

Corrigenda to OECD publications may be found on line at: *www.oecd.org/about/publishing/corrigenda.htm*.
© OECD 2017

You can copy, download or print OECD content for your own use, and you can include excerpts from OECD publications, databases and multimedia products in your own documents, presentations, blogs, websites and teaching materials, provided that suitable acknowledgement of OECD as source and copyright owner is given. All requests for public or commercial use and translation rights should be submitted to *rights@oecd.org*. Requests for permission to photocopy portions of this material for public or commercial use shall be addressed directly to the Copyright Clearance Center (CCC) at *info@copyright.com* or the Centre français d'exploitation du droit de copie (CFC) at *contact@cfcopies.com*.

Foreword

Whenever producing formal guidance and standards in various areas of public governance – such as open data, public procurement or regulatory policy – the OECD often follows through with a less formal, more practically-minded "toolkit" to allow users to go beyond the level of principles to action and impact.

In the area of budget transparency, a different approach is called for. This is an area which is already well served with official standards, guidance manuals, and a wealth of other resources providing inspiring country examples. In such circumstances, rather than provide guidance to the OECD principles alone, a larger goal is to help users by raising their awareness of the various standards and guidelines that are available, how these materials complement one another, and how they can best be selected and applied to achieve the overall objective of a more open, transparent, inclusive and accountable budget process.

Accordingly, the OECD has designed this Budget Transparency Toolkit with the participation and collaboration of the broader global community of budget and fiscal transparency institutions – in particular the International Monetary Fund (IMF), the World Bank Group, the International Budget Partnership (IBP), the International Federation of Accountants (IFAC), and the Public Expenditure and Financial Accountability (PEFA) Program – all of which form part of the Global Initiative of Fiscal Transparency (GIFT) Network. The Toolkit does not aim to repeat or replace any of the materials that are already available from these bodies; it simply aims to serve as a guide or signpost to these materials, while also reinforcing some key practical messages about budget and fiscal transparency.

The Toolkit is accordingly structured in two chapters. **Chapter 1** serves as a direct introduction or gateway to the various institutions, official instruments and guidance materials, including standards issued by international organisations after extensive consultation with relevant stakeholders and public. The purpose of Chapter 1 is to give users a sense of their purpose and structure, and of how these resources can best be put to use.

Chapter 2 provides an alternative way of navigating to the various standards and guidance materials, by using a structure - developed by the OECD - based around five key institutional or sectoral areas. This section includes direct cross-references to the various international standards and guidance materials and helps to underline the broad common ground that exists in the area of budget and fiscal transparency. Chapter 2 also features some "suggested starting points" or key orientation messages to help users in understanding the issues involved. These "suggested starting points" are put forward for illustrative purposes by the OECD and should not be seen as "shortcuts" through the official standards issued by the various institutions. The OECD is grateful for the co-operation and advice of the international community of budget and fiscal transparency organisations, which have kindly allowed us to make reference to their materials in the interests of making this Toolkit as useful as possible.

Table of Contents

Preface 7
Introduction 9

Chapter 1 Gateway to international standards and guidance on budget and fiscal transparency 13

Overview of budget and fiscal transparency: The international landscape 15
The G20 17
Global Initiative for Fiscal Transparency (GIFT) 18
International Budget Partnership (IBP) 20
International Federation of Accountants (IFAC) and the International Public Sector Accounting Standards Board (IPSASB) 23
International Monetary Fund (IMF) 26
Organisation for Economic Co-operation and Development (OECD) 29
Public Expenditure and Financial Accountability (PEFA) 32
World Bank Group 35
Other relevant organisations 37

Chapter 2 Applying Budget Transparency in different areas: OECD guidance on topics and resources 39

Navigating the international standards and guidance table 41
Multi-dimensional Map of Budget Transparency 43
Clear budget information from government 45
Parliamentary scrutiny and engagement 61
Independent oversight and control 69
Openness and civic engagement 77
Promoting integrity with the private sector 87
Annex: Transparency throughout the budget cycle 99

Preface

by

Juan Pablo Guerrero

Network Director, Global Initiative for Fiscal Transparency

Budget transparency brings many benefits for citizens and for society. Openness, trust and public accountability are among these benefits. Increasingly, fostering budget transparency is also seen as vital to promoting integrity in public governance and strengthening anti-corruption policies.

However, putting budget transparency into practice can sometimes appear as a daunting task: Where should a country begin in implementing a reform agenda? Where should citizens and civil society organisations focus their efforts, to make a meaningful impact in realising these potential benefits?

In fact, until the mid-1990s there was no internationally-recognised definition of fiscal transparency or budget transparency and no codification of what these terms comprised. Since that time a number of international institutions have developed standards, guidelines and assessment tools to promote greater openness in public finance management. The main international instruments have been revised extensively since 2014. The production by the OECD of this *Budget Transparency Toolkit, with Practical Steps for Supporting Openness, Integrity and Accountability in Public Financial Management* is therefore timely and very pertinent. It is a way to introduce practitioners to the various standards and guidelines that are available, help them understand how these materials complement each other and allow users to go beyond the level of principles and theory, to action and impact. The Toolkit is an important contribution to disseminating and standardising recognised good practices in budget and fiscal transparency to those inside and outside governments around the world. And this makes it a very valuable tool in promoting open, responsive government and in supporting global anti-corruption efforts.

We welcome the OECD's introduction of this *Budget Transparency Toolkit* with the participation and collaboration of the broader global community of budget and fiscal transparency institutions, including the International Monetary Fund, the World Bank Group, the International Budget Partnership, the International Federation of Accountants and the Public Expenditure and Financial Assessment Program, all of which are members of the Global Initiative of Fiscal Transparency (GIFT) Network, along with the OECD itself. The Toolkit both reflects and illustrates the increasing consensus about what constitutes good practice in openness about how public money is raised and spent. Increasingly, the various international instruments recognise the diversity of country contexts by setting graduated standards rather than stipulating a single set of practices. The reader has a very useful tool to serve as a guide to basic questions and crucial issues, while also reinforcing some key practical messages about budget and fiscal transparency, drawn from this extensive international corpus of material. For example, the Toolkit defines 'openness and civic engagement' as one of the five elements in its organising framework, reflecting the most current insights into this important aspect of modern budgeting.

The GIFT network is pleased to have worked with the OECD in producing this Toolkit. The Toolkit illustrates one of GIFT's objectives in action: the promotion of more comprehensive and coherent efforts to extend fiscal transparency in pursuit of the GIFT High Level Principles on Fiscal Transparency, Participation and Accountability. It is especially important that the Toolkit acknowledges that citizens and taxpayers need to be placed at the core of efforts to increase transparency and accountability for the management of public resources. Opening up budgets and public financial management, and providing spaces for direct citizen engagement, can reduce corruption and waste, and increase the odds of taxes being used to deliver quality public services and to achieve real improvements in living standards and in social, economic and environmental outcomes. As such, this Toolkit is a meaningful response and a very valuable contribution to the search for practical and innovative solutions to today's challenges of open, transparent and inclusive budgeting.

Introduction

Good budgeting is supported by, and in turn supports, the various pillars of modern public governance: transparency, integrity, openness, participation, accountability and a strategic approach to planning and achieving national objectives

- OECD Recommendation on Budgetary Governance

The principle of budget transparency - including the clarity, comprehensiveness, reliability, timeliness and accessibility of public reporting on public finances - is now widely accepted around the world. There are various definitions of budget transparency and fiscal transparency, but they can all be summarised in one core concept: **budget transparency means being fully open with people about how public money is raised and used.**

There are multiple reasons why budget transparency is seen as a desirable objective. Here are some of the most important recognised benefits of budget transparency:

Accountability: Clarity about the use of public funds is necessary so that public representatives and officials can be accountable for effectiveness and efficiency.

Integrity: Public spending is vulnerable not only to waste and misuse, but also to fraud. "Sunlight is the best policy" for preventing corruption and maintaining high standards of integrity in the use of public funds.

Inclusiveness: Budget decisions can profoundly affect the interests and living standards of different people and groups in society; transparency involves an informed and inclusive debate about the budget policy impacts.

Trust: An open and transparent budget process fosters trust in society that people's views and interests are respected and that public money is used well.

Quality: Transparent and inclusive budgeting supports better fiscal outcomes and more responsive, impactful and equitable public policies.

The role of a "Toolkit on Budget Transparency"

Many international organisations, public and private, have devoted attention to budget transparency over the years. Together, they comprise the international community of practitioners, experts and advocates, with a range of complementary perspectives (see Chapter 1). Most of these organisations have produced detailed analysis and guidance on budget transparency issues. The purpose of this document is not to repeat or replace all of that guidance. Instead, it is intended that this Toolkit will serve three purposes:

1. Provide a gateway to the wealth of information, including official standards issued by international bodies with wide representation, detailed guidance and other resources on budget and fiscal transparency that are available across the international community

2. Help countries make best use of this material to self-assess their own level of budget transparency, or encourage assessments through third parties such as International Financial Institutions (IFIs), and to plan and implement an agenda of transparency-focused reform, by providing a useful digest and "checklist" of common lessons from the international experience

3. Bring together, in a collaborative way, the insights of the international community of budget and fiscal transparency so as to reinforce key messages and priorities.

By helping countries to take action on budget transparency and by pointing them towards the additional practical supports that are most relevant, in light of country-specific circumstances, this Toolkit can be a practical resource and point of reference.

How can I use the "tools" in this Toolkit?

For countries wishing to improve their budget transparency levels, there is much authoritative guidance available on the standards that should be followed, and how they should be applied across different phases of the budget cycle, from its preparation and planning stages, through to presentation, debate, authorisation, execution, reporting and accountability. There are also many resources available in a range of formats – from user-friendly to highly technical and in-depth – aimed at different practitioners and users of budget data. Not surprisingly, it can sometimes seem difficult to know where exactly to start. To help in making the best use of this material, and in deciding upon the most suitable approach for your country or institution, the following tools are provided.

Gateway to official standards and guidelines (Chapter 1): All of the official standards, legal instruments and key guidance documents relating to budget and fiscal transparency, from all of the relevant international organisations, are presented in **Chapter 1** of the Toolkit. The particular characteristics and roles of these standards / guidelines are explained, so that users of the Toolkit can decide which may be most relevant for your own purposes; and guidance is provided on how to start making use of these materials. The official standards and guidelines form the foundation on which this Toolkit is based: After gaining an introduction to the various dimensions of budget transparency provided throughout this Toolkit, users can refer directly to these materials for more detailed and definitive guidance.

Multi-dimensional map of budget transparency (Chapter 2): Depending on the institutions or sectors of most interest to users, different standards and guidance materials will be of relevance. The multi-dimensional map of budget transparency - see page 43 - is designed to help users navigate directly to the resources available in each area. The five key dimensions, based on the structure developed by OECD for **Chapter 2** of the Toolkit, are as follows:

- the government (or executive branch)
- the parliament (or legislature)
- independent public institutions (including audit offices and fiscal councils)
- citizens and civil society organisations, and
- the private sector.

Toolkit Topics: The multi-dimensional approach is used as a way of structuring the guidance material throughout Chapter 2 of the Toolkit. For each of the five dimensions, a number of particular budget transparency 'topics' are set out in a standard format.

- Each individual **Toolkit Topic** is first identified, by letter and number, with an outline of its role and importance for budget transparency.

- Some ⌲ **suggested starting points** within each Topic are then listed in summary form. These points provide an initial orientation on key areas for action on budget transparency, drawn from the more detailed international standards - they should not, however, be regarded as a substitute for the standards themselves. In addition, different items may sometimes be of greater or lesser relevance depending on country-specific circumstances.

➢ **Navigating to the international standards:** Each Topic concludes with an indication of where it is dealt with more fully in the ✦ **International Standards and Guidance**[*]. The various international norms and guidance materials are referenced through simple "tags" (as explained at the end of this introductory chapter). In this way, the Shared Toolkit serves as a "navigation aid" to the existing standards and guidance material, pointing the way to the detailed and authoritative material to help users take the next steps in putting budget transparency into practice.

➢ Beneath each of the Topics, you will find 🌐 **Examples from around the world** which, are brief illustrations of how various countries have succeeded in implementing the particular budget transparency tool or topic. The country examples are not limited to OECD countries, but include innovative and inspiring examples from every region.

➢ **Budget cycle action points:** The Annex (see page 99) shows cross-references from the Toolkit Topics to the distinct phases of the budget cycle, and to the (potential) roles of various institutions at each phase.

Through this common, structured approach, it is hoped that users of the Toolkit can get a good sense of the most important issues in each broad area; identify actions that can be taken to improve budget transparency; and easily find their way towards more international examples, standards and practical guidance.

---

[*] International standards are those standards that *i)* have been issued by an internationally recognised body (with wide representation of countries), *ii)* have broad applicability across different jurisdictions (widely applicable across countries), and *iii)* have been broadly endorsed through extensive consultation with relevant stakeholders, including a public consultation process.

Chapter 1

Gateway to international standards and guidance on budget and fiscal transparency

There are many international bodies active in the area of budget and fiscal transparency. This chapter introduces the key international bodies and explains how their instruments and resources can be used by budget practitioners and stakeholders.

Overview of budget and fiscal transparency: The international landscape

Several international organisations provide official standards on budget and fiscal transparency, and there are a range of other bodies – inter-governmental groups, civil society organisations, professional bodies and others – that provide additional information and guidance. All share a common cause of promoting higher levels of transparency in the financial affairs of government and public bodies; however users of this information can sometimes find it difficult to understand how the different standards and guidance materials fit together and can be used.

In this **Chapter 1** of the Budget Transparency Toolkit, after an initial outline of how the various institutions and instruments complement one another, each of the key instruments is introduced and explained. **Chapter 2** of the Toolkit provides alternative routes to finding the official instruments as they apply in particular areas, along with practical orientations and suggestions about their application.

Budget and Fiscal Transparency – the evolution of a concept

Until the mid-1990s there was no internationally-recognised definition of budget transparency / fiscal transparency and no codification of what it comprised. Prompted by lessons learned from the East Asia financial crisis of the time, the International Monetary Fund (IMF) introduced in 1998 a *Code of Good Practices on Fiscal Transparency*, and in the following year started assessing country practices against the code. The OECD's 2002 *Best Practices in Budget Transparency* focused on the central government budget sector in advanced countries. The Public Sector Committee of International Federation of Accountants initiated the *International Public Sector Accounting Standards (IPSAS)* project in 1996, and by 2002 had issued a core set of accounting standards for the public sector.

Subsequently, the 2002 multi-stakeholder *Extractive Industries Transparency Initiative (EITI)* and the IMF's *Guide on Resource Revenue Transparency* (2005) reflected heightened concern over fiscal transparency in countries dependent on extractive industries. The multi-stakeholder *Public Expenditure and Financial Accountability* (PEFA) reports that commenced in 2005, on the other hand, have been most widely used in lower and middle income countries.

The International Budget Partnership introduced the bi-annual Open Budget Survey in 2006, providing an independent civil society assessment of budget transparency and generating quantitative data on levels and trends in budget transparency.

The global financial crisis from 2008, together with concern about the slow and uneven pace of improvements in fiscal transparency, prompted a re-thinking of the overall approach as well as revisions to many of the instruments. A number of international organisations and other stakeholders formed the Global Initiative for Fiscal Transparency in 2011, which issued a set of High Level Principles on Fiscal Transparency, Participation and Accountability the following year to promote more comprehensive and coherent efforts to extend transparency, as well as a new element of direct public participation in fiscal policy design and implementation.

Over the last few years many of the instruments referred to above have been revised and updated. In particular:

- the **IMF** released a completely restructured Fiscal Transparency Code in 2014 and a new assessment tool, the Fiscal Transparency Evaluation (FTE)
- the **OECD** issued a new set of *Principles of Budgetary Governance* the following year to complement and build upon the 2002 *Best Practices*
- a revised **PEFA** indicator set was released in 2016
- the **IPSAS** standards have been expanded under the independent International Public Sector Accounting Standards Board (IPSASB), which is facilitated by IFAC. They now comprise a comprehensive set of accrual-based standards for the preparation of general purpose financial statements by governments and other public sector entities around the world*; and
- from 2017 the **IBP's** Open Budget Survey 2017 is completed against a revised set of questions.

Increasingly these instruments recognise the diversity of country contexts by setting graduated standards rather than stipulating a single set of practices. The instruments also, to different degrees, incorporate principles that acknowledge the public's right to participate in deliberation over the design and implementation of fiscal policies, which reflects the increasing importance of putting the public at the centre of the management of public resources. In parallel, the G20 has sought to draw upon the international work on budget and fiscal transparency in order to support other important pillars of good governance, including anti-corruption.

Over time, the terms fiscal and budget transparency have become increasingly broad umbrella terms that subsume a number of dimensions and topics. They cover both the supply side - governments, and increasingly non-state actors also, publishing information - and the demand side - legislatures, civil society, and other stakeholders seeking to use information to hold government actors accountable and to participate more directly in public debate over resource allocation. Fiscal transparency incorporates open budgeting, the delivery of tax-funded public services, public procurement, public infrastructure projects, financial and non-financial reporting, the management of public assets and liabilities, and activities at the boundary of the government sector, such as public corporations and Public Private Partnerships. Finally, the concepts and tools of budget and fiscal transparency are also being applied to subnational governments.

In formal terms, some of these instruments are official international standards (e.g. the IMF Fiscal Transparency Code) or form part of the international law for various countries (e.g. OECD Principles of Budgetary Governance); while others are authoritative guidance instruments, *de facto* standards or internationally-recognised assessment tools. In recent years there has been an explicit attempt by the different institutions responsible for these instruments to achieve more consistency and coherence across them while recognising that they each serve somewhat different purposes. **This Toolkit is a further step to highlight what the various instruments have in common, and helps budget practitioners and users in applying these standards in order to improve budget and fiscal transparency levels.**

* It should be noted that several countries employ cash rather than accrual accounting for public financial reporting. Of countries employing accrual accounting, nearly all develop national accounting standards and many use international standards such as IPSAS as a reference.

The G20

The **G20** was initiated in 1999 as a forum of the 20 largest economies in the world, to lead action on key issues for global economic co-operation and good governance. G20 countries are: Argentina, Australia, Brazil, Canada, China, France, Germany, India, Indonesia, Italy, Japan, Republic of Korea, Mexico, Russia, Saudi Arabia, South Africa, Turkey, United Kingdom, United States, and the European Union. International bodies such as the IMF, OECD and World Bank are also invited to attend G20 summits. The G20 draws upon expertise from its members and international organisations to spearhead progress in areas such as infrastructure, open data and anti-corruption.

The **G20 Anti-Corruption Action Plan 2017-18** (adopted in September 2016 under China's Presidency of the G20) notes that "Government spending is vitally important to our economies and can be vulnerable to corruption," and that "transparency is key to deterring and uncovering corruption." The G20 therefore aims to promote greater transparency in budget processes and public contracting, including through greater citizen engagement, use of open data and improved coordination among international organisations. The **Anti-Corruption Working Group (ACWG)** of G20 is responsible for driving forward and implementing this agenda, encouraging a deeper understanding of how budget transparency can support, and be integrated within, broader anti-corruption frameworks.

Other relevant G20 instruments are:

➢ **G20 Anti-corruption Open Data Principles (2014)** which form the foundation for access to, release and use of open government data to strengthen the fight against corruption. The Principles recognise that open data provides a platform to help expand social participation and enhance co-responsibility in areas such as public procurement, political financing standards, and fiscal and budget transparency.

➢ **G20 Guiding Principles on Integrity in Public Procurement (2015)** which note that public procurement represents a large share of G20 countries' economies - 13% of GDP on average – and that financial management controls and other safeguards are necessary to ensure integrity and value-for-money.

ⓘ **How and why to use?** The G20 instruments are not formal legal standards but represent clear political commitments on behalf of G20 governments, and as such they serve as important channels for co-ordinating international policy. By aligning national policies and strategies with the G20 instruments, countries – whether or not they are members of the G20 – can add momentum to global efforts to improve public governance in critical areas.

Quick link: **http://g20.org**

Global Initiative for Fiscal Transparency (GIFT)

The **Global Initiative for Fiscal Transparency (GIFT)** was founded in 2011 as a multi-stakeholder action network to advance fiscal transparency, participation, and accountability in countries around the world. GIFT's founding Lead Stewards are the World Bank, the IMF, the International Budget Partnership (IBP), and the Departments/Secretaries of budget of the governments of Brazil and the Philippines. The International Federation of Accountants subsequently joined as a sixth Lead Steward in 2014. Two dozen other official, civil society organisations and donor agencies are stewards of GIFT, including the OECD (see www.fiscaltransparency.net for further details). Since, 2013, GIFT is hosted at IBP and funded by the World Bank, the William & Flora Hewlett Foundation and the Omidyar Network.

The basic motivation for establishing GIFT was that the overall state of budget transparency around the world is poor: Measured against the Open Budget Index, the national budgets of 77 countries - home to half the world's population - were at that time failing to meet basic standards of budget transparency. While there had been some progress in increasing fiscal transparency, it was uneven and slow, and would take a generation to achieve significant and sustainable improvement in many countries. The Global Financial Crisis had also revealed basic weaknesses in fiscal transparency, and prompted a fundamental re-thinking of the approach (see for instance the 2012 IMF paper, Fiscal Transparency, Accountability, and Risk).

GIFT was formed to bring about a step-increase in government openness by bringing multiple stakeholders together to address the challenges in a new and more co-ordinated manner. It has four main work streams: strengthening incentives; advancing global norms; technical assistance and capacity building; and harnessing new technologies.

One of the network's first actions was to develop a new set of *High Level Principles of Fiscal Transparency, Participation and Accountability*. As illustrated in the figure below, these are designed to sit above the existing set of international standards, norms, and assessment instruments, to promote increased coherence across those instruments, and to promote the development of new instruments where there are gaps.

The GIFT High Level Principles were endorsed by the United Nations General Assembly (UNGA) in 2012, which encouraged member states to 'intensify efforts to enhance transparency, participation and accountability in fiscal policies, including through the consideration of the principles set out by GIFT.'

www.un.org/ga/search/view_doc.asp?symbol=A/RES/67/218&Lang=E

High Level Principle 10 asserts a public right to direct public participation in the formulation and implementation of fiscal policy. Given the limited guidance on how public entities should engage directly with the public in managing public resources, GIFT embarked on a substantial multi-year work programme to generate greater knowledge about country practices and recent innovations in citizen engagement. GIFT has completed eight country case studies of public participation in fiscal policy, has developed a set of *Principles of Public Participation in Fiscal Policy,* and will be publishing a Guide to this potentially transformative new field in December 2016.

Requirements for public participation have recently been incorporated in the 2014 IMF Fiscal Transparency Code and in the OECD's Principles of Budgetary Governance 2014, and the 2017 Open Budget Survey includes an expanded section on public participation that fully reflects the GIFT *Participation Principles.* GIFT has also developed an indicator measuring public participation in fiscal policy that is being piloted as a voluntary supplement in a PEFA assessment.

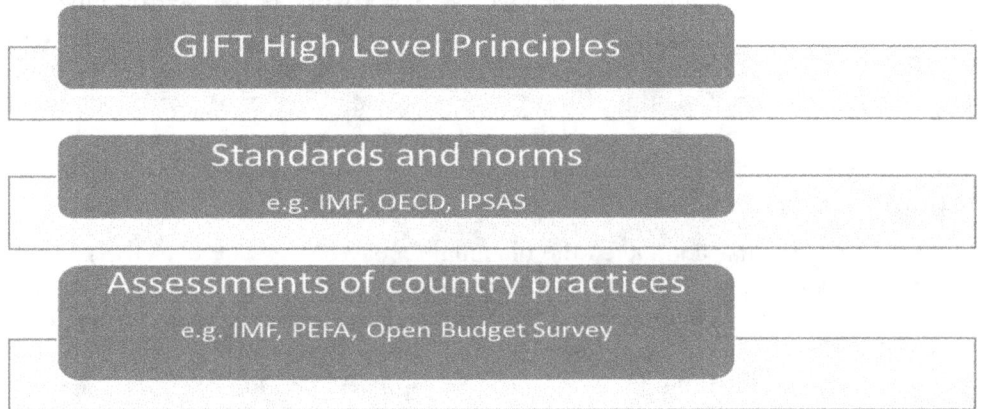

GIFT initiated the establishment of the Fiscal Openness Working Group (FOWG) of the Open Government Partnership at the London OGP Summit in 2013(www.fiscaltransparency.net/fowg/). The FOWG, which is convened by GIFT, supports and promotes the implementation of more ambitious budget and fiscal transparency commitments made by OGP governments. It does this through peer-to-peer learning and exchange of experience between officials; by bringing government officials and civil society budget experts together to discuss transparency and openness reforms in their countries and regions; and by assessing progress in implementing fiscal transparency commitments in OGP Action Plans and commenting on draft Action Plans.

GIFT's work on harnessing new technologies has focused on developing a global tool for publishing budget information in open data format. This has involved working with Open Knowledge to develop a technical platform, with the World Bank's BOOST tool (providing budget data), and with governments including those of Brazil and Mexico to test the tool. In September 2016 Mexico became the first government to publish its budget in open data format, drawing on GIFT support.

GIFT has also published considerable research on the evidence for the causes and effects of fiscal openness, including case studies, meta evaluations, and research on incentives.

International Budget Partnership (IBP)

The **International Budget Partnership (IBP)** was formed in 1997 to advocate for transparent, inclusive, and accountable government budget processes as a means to improve governance and reduce global poverty. IBP's work is focused on citizens and civil society, and includes: strengthening the skills and knowledge of country-based civil society organisations; researching and monitoring the status of budget transparency, participation, and accountability around the world; engaging with international stakeholders to encourage them to play a greater role in budget issues; and building rigorous evidence to measure governments progress in becoming more open as well as the impact of IBP and its partners to inform more strategic and effective practices.

➢ Since 2006 IBP has conducted the biannual Open Budget Survey (OBS), a unique, global, independent, and comparable measure of government practices in budget transparency, participation, and oversight. The **Open Budget Survey 2015** examined 102 countries, and its next iteration (in 2017) will cover 115 countries. This makes the OBS the biggest and most regularly conducted cross-country time series on how openly national/central governments manage public finances. The data are collected through the **Open Budget Survey Questionnaire**, which includes a total of 142 questions and guidelines on three pillars of the accountability system:

- **Budget transparency:** The public availability, timeliness, and comprehensiveness of eight key budget documents that, according to internationally accepted good practice criteria for public financial management, all countries should publish at different points in the budget process. This section of the survey is used to calculate the **Open Budget Index**, whereby countries are given a score between 0 and 100 and ranked according to their level of budget transparency.

- **Budget participation:** The opportunities governments are providing to civil society and the general public to engage in the budget process, in order to contribute and influence decisions on how public resources are raised and spent.

- **Budget oversight:** The role and effectiveness of formal institutions (independent fiscal institutions, legislatures, and supreme audit institutions) to understand, monitor, and influence how public resources are being raised and spent.

Many of the criteria used in the OBS are drawn from those developed by multilateral organisations, such as the IMF's **Code of Good Practices on Fiscal Transparency**, the Public Expenditure and Financial Accountability initiative (PEFA), the OECD's **Best**

Practices for Fiscal Transparency, and the International Organisation of Supreme Audit Institutions' **Lima Declaration of Guidelines of Supreme Audit Precepts.**

> ⓘ How and why to use? The OBS is designed to be easily understood by a broad audience. It provides clear assessment criteria through the indicators/questions and guidelines that are included in the Open Budget Questionnaire, such as a specific and measurable definition of "public availability of information." In all countries assessed, the OBS questionnaires are completed and reviewed by independent budget experts that are not affiliated to the government, or to any political party. In addition, the OBS questions are evidence-based and require citations and explanatory comments in order for answers to be accepted. This makes the OBS a uniquely independent and unbiased collection of information on the status of fiscal openness around the world. The survey results are publicly available and can therefore be used by anyone who wishes to identify trends, progress, and fall-backs at the national, regional, and global level. Development agencies, civil society organisations, and government officials have used the results to find concrete ways to improve budget transparency. By honing in on specific indicators and graded responses, country-level policy makers can diagnose weaknesses, identify gaps, and develop strategies for making the budget more open.
>
> **Quick link:** www.internationalbudget.org/publications/open-budget-survey-2017-guide-questionnaire-english/
>
> **Explore** the Open Budget Survey results here: http://survey.internationalbudget.org/

IBP also produces guides and research that expand on some of the elements assessed in the Open Budget Survey, most notably:

> ➤ The Power of Making It Simple provides step-by-step guidance to governments on producing a Citizens Budget and includes suggestions on how to meet challenges that often arise in the process. This is complemented by a dedicated section of the IBP's website which provides resources on how to develop a Citizens Budget, a wealth of examples, and some considerations on the importance of this document for showing a government's institutionalised commitment to ensure citizens have a firm understanding of the many ways the budget affects their lives.
>
> **Quick link:** www.internationalbudget.org/opening-budgets/citizens-budgets/

➢ **Guide to Transparency in Government Budget Reports**: This guide responds to the questions of "why are budget reports important?" and "what should they include?" It supports governments in their efforts to meet international standards of good practice on budget transparency by explaining what key reports and documents they should be producing and making available throughout the budget process, what information should be in those reports, and providing examples of model documents from other countries. The guide covers each of the eight key budget documents: the Pre-Budget Statement, the Executive's Budget Proposal, the Citizens Budget, the Enacted Budget, In-Year Reports, the Mid-Year Review, the Year-End Report, and the Audit Report.

Quick link: www.internationalbudget.org/publications/guide-to-transparency-in-government-budget-reports-why-are-budget-reports-important-and-what-should-they-include/

International Federation of Accountants (IFAC) and the International Public Sector Accounting Standards Board (IPSASB)

The International Federation of Accountants (IFAC) is the global organisation for the accountancy profession dedicated to serving the public interest by strengthening the profession and contributing to the development of strong international economies. Founded in 1977, IFAC is composed of more than 175 members and associates in more than 130 countries and jurisdictions, representing almost 3 million accountants in public practice, education, government service, industry, and commerce.

Together with its member organisation, the Chartered Institute of Public Finance and Accountancy (CIPFA), IFAC has developed the *International Framework: Good Governance in the Public Sector* (2014), to encourage more effective public sector governance. The Framework specifically emphasises that strong financial management, and the financial discipline it engenders, are essential for the implementation of public sector policies as they facilitate strategic resource allocation, efficient service delivery, greater accountability, and better outcomes for all citizens.

To catalyse collaboration and stronger public financial management globally, IFAC launched the Accountability. Now. initiative, which strives for higher standards of public sector information around the world. It challenges governments to recognise the importance of working toward financial reporting that meets international accrual-based standards known as IPSAS. Its goal is to support governments around the world in making better decisions and becoming more transparent and accountable. Enhanced public financial accounting and reporting is essential to addressing the problems highlighted by global economic and fiscal crises. It informs government policy and helps to make public services - and economies - more sustainable and resilient over the long term.

Additionally, IFAC has developed the following resources, relevant for the activities discussed in this Toolkit:

- *From Bolt-on to Built-in Managing Risk as an Integral Part of Managing an Organisation* (2015) positions risk management and internal control as it was originally intended - as a highly relevant and useful process that supports organisational decision making and long-term success.

- *Principles for Effective Business Reporting Processes* (2013) presents 11 key principles along with practical implementation guidance to help professional accountants in business, and their organisations, evaluate and improve their business reporting processes and generate higher-quality financial information.

- *Evaluating and Improving Internal Control in Organisations* (2012) guides professional accountants in business and organisations in continuously evaluating and improving internal control, ensuring it plays an integral role in their governance and risk management systems.

IFAC also supports four independent standard-setting boards, among them, the **International Public Sector Accounting Standards Board (IPSASB)**, which develops IPSAS, accrual-based standards used for the preparation of general purpose financial statements by governments and other public sector entities around the world. Through these standards, the IPSASB aims to enhance the quality, consistency and transparency of public sector financial reporting worldwide. It also issues guidance, facilitates the exchange of information among accountants and others who work in the public sector, and promotes the acceptance of, and international convergence to, IPSAS.

The IPSASB has a single strategic objective: Strengthening public financial management and knowledge globally through increasing adoption of accrual-based IPSAS by:

1. Developing high-quality public sector financial reporting standards;

2. Developing other publications for the public sector; and

3. Raising awareness of IPSAS and the benefits of their adoption.

As of December 1, 2016 the IPSASB had issued 39 IPSAS (four withdrawn or in the process of being withdrawn), an IPSAS for the cash basis of accounting, and three Recommended Practice Guidelines dealing with the broader aspects of financial reporting outside the financial statements. In late 2014 the IPSASB published the first global public sector Conceptual Framework.

Established in 2015, the Public Interest Committee (PIC) of IPSASB provides oversight of IPSASB's standard-setting activities and ensures that those activities are in the public interest. The PIC is currently composed of representatives from the International Monetary Fund, International Organisation of Supreme Audit Institutions (INTOSAI), Organisation for Economic Co-operation and Development (OECD), and the World Bank Group. The PIC provides recommendations on:

- The IPSASB's terms of reference;

- The arrangements for nomination and appointment of IPSASB members; and

- The procedures and processes for developing the IPSASB's strategy, work plan, and IPSAS.

The Consultative Advisory Group (CAG) is an integral and important part of the IPSASB's formal process of consultation. Representatives of CAG member organisations provide advice on:

- The IPSASB's strategy, work program and agenda, including project priorities;

- IPSASB's projects, including views on key technical issues or matters that may impede the adoption or effective implementation of IPSAS™; and

- Other matters of relevance to the standard-setting activities of the IPSASB.

The CAG's first meeting was in Toronto in June 2016.

International Monetary Fund (IMF)

The **International Monetary Fund (IMF) was founded in 1944 and currently has a membership of 189 countries.** The IMF's mandate is to *i)* ensure the stability of the international financial system and promote sustainable growth by reviewing national, regional and global economic and financial developments through policy dialogue known as surveillance; *ii)* provide financial assistance to countries with balance of payments needs; and *iii)* support capacity building in member countries through technical assistance and training, including in the fiscal area.

How does the IMF promote fiscal transparency?

The IMF's Fiscal Transparency Code (FTC), part of the *IMF's Fiscal Transparency Initiative*, is the global standard for disclosure of information about public finances. The FTC provides a set of principles to improve fiscal transparency and accountability, to support policymaking, enhance fiscal management and strengthen policy dialogue. The FTC was first adopted in 1998 and has been twice revised in 2007 and 2014.[1] The 2014 FTC comprises a set of principles built around four "pillars" (see figure below) that reflect the IMF's focus on macro-critical issues:

- **Pillar 1: Fiscal Reporting**, to offer relevant, comprehensive, timely, and reliable information on the government's financial position and performance.

- **Pillar II: Fiscal Forecasting and Budgeting,** to provide a clear statement of the government's budgetary objectives and policy intentions, together with comprehensive, timely, and credible projections of the evolution of public finances.

- **Pillar III: Fiscal Risk Analysis and Management,** to ensure that risks to the public finances are disclosed, analysed, and managed, and that fiscal decision-making across the public sector is effectively coordinated.

- **Pillar IV: Resource Revenue Management,** to provide a transparent framework for the ownership, contracting, taxation, and utilisation of natural resource endowments.[2]

Four Pillars of the IMF Fiscal Transparency Code

I. FISCAL REPORTING	II. FISCAL FORECASTING & BUDGETING	III. FISCAL RISK ANALYSIS & MANAGEMENT	IV. RESOURCE REVENUE MANAGEMENT
1.1 Coverage	2.1 Comprehensiveness	3.1 Risk Analysis and Disclosure	4.1 Ownership, Contracting & Financial Regime
1.2 Frequency and Timelines	2.2 Orderliness	3.2 Risk Management	4.2 Financial Reporting
1.3 Quality	2.3 Policy Orientation		4.3 Financial Forecasting & Budgeting
1.4 Integrity	2.4 Credibility	3.3 Fiscal Co-ordination	4.4 Fiscal Risk Analysis & Management

The FTC was developed in a participatory manner, with review by main partners in the transparency community, including international and civil society organisations. It reflects recent advances in international standards, and emphasises the quality of published information, the importance of fiscal risks, while taking account of different levels of country capacity. For each transparency principle, the FTC differentiates between basic, good, and advanced practices to provide countries with clear milestones toward full compliance with the FTC and ensure its applicability to the full range of IMF member countries.

How and why to use the Code?

Fiscal Transparency Evaluations (FTEs) assess country practices against the FTC (replacing the previous Fiscal ROSCs (Report on the Observance of Standards and Codes). FTEs provide countries with a comprehensive assessment of their fiscal transparency practices, quantify the fiscal risks that they face, and set out a sequenced and prioritised action plan to meet good transparency practices as set out by the FTC.

FTEs are carried out at the request of countries, and form part of the IMF's ongoing policy dialogue and capacity building efforts. Several FTEs, across a broad spectrum of IMF member countries, have been completed (see http://www.imf.org/external/np/fad/trans/).[3]

What are other complementary tools?

The IMF has also developed other diagnostic tools in the fiscal area to complement the FTC, all of which include questions relating to transparency in their specific fields. IMF staff have worked with other stakeholders to ensure that the standards and guidelines in the area of fiscal transparency are fully aligned, and send a consistent and mutually reinforcing message. These complementary tools include the following:

- **Government Finance Statistics Manual (GFSM), 2014**, the international standard for compiling and disseminating government finance statistics, including for publication in the IMF GFS Yearbook (see www.imf.org/external/Pubs/FT/GFS/Manual/2014/gfsfinal.pdf).

- **Public-Private Partnerships Fiscal Risks Assessment Model (PFRAM)**, an analytical tool to assess the potential fiscal costs and risks arising from Public-Private Partnership (PPP) projects (see www.imf.org/external/np/fad/publicinvestment/index.htm#4).

- **Public Investment Management Assessment (PIMA)** instrument, which evaluates 15 institutions that shape decision-making at the three key stages of the public investment cycle: *planning* sustainable investment across the public sector; *allocating* investment to the right sectors and projects; and *implementing* projects on time and on budget (see www.imf.org/external/np/fad/publicinvestment/index.htm#3).

- **Public Expenditure and Financial Accountability (PEFA)** (jointly with other partners), a tool that helps governments assess public financial management (PFM) practices.

- **Tax Administration Diagnostic Assessment Tool (TADAT)** (jointly with other partners), which is designed to provide an objective assessment of the health of key components of a country's system of tax administration (see www.tadat.org/overview/overview.html).

What to expect next?

- Complete Pillar IV of the FTC and submit the full FTC to the IMF Board for approval.

- Finalise a two-volume Fiscal Transparency Manual, which will provide more detailed guidance on the implementation of the Code's principles and practices. Volume I will cover Pillars I, II, and III, and Volume II will focus on Pillar IV.

Notes

1. Two IMF Board papers explain the ongoing work on fiscal transparency: a 2012 paper on "Fiscal Transparency, Accountability, and Risk"; and a 2014 paper on "Update on the Fiscal Transparency Initiative" (available at www.imf.org/external/np/fad/trans/).

2. This pillar is still under development. A draft of Pillar IV has already undergone two rounds of public consultation and is being piloted in the field.

3. By November 2016, 19 FTEs have been carried of which 14 are published; about 10 more are in the pipeline.

Organisation for Economic Co-operation and Development (OECD)

The **Organisation for Economic Co-operation and Development (OECD)** was founded in 1961 to promote "better policies for better lives" in economic development and across a wide range of sectoral areas such as education and health; as well as dealing with tax co-operation, public sector integrity, infrastructure, budgeting and digital government. Key themes and priorities for OECD work are the well-being of citizens, inclusive growth, and trust in government.

In the area of public financial management, the OECD convenes the peer network of **Senior Budget Officials (the SBO)** and its regional sister networks, which discuss best practices and contribute to standard-setting. International standards and guidance materials produced by the OECD include:

> **Best Practices for Budget Transparency (2002)**: The Best Practices define budget transparency as "the full disclosure of all relevant fiscal information in a timely and systematic manner", and take a three-fold approach to the subject. *First*, **seven main budget-related reports** are outlined and described. *Second*, **"specific disclosures"** are outlined – in other words, various types of information (such as economic assumptions, financial assets and liabilities, and contingent liabilities) which should be included in budget reports. *Third*, important issues of **integrity, control and accountability** are outlined, including clear accounting policies, internal control processes, reports from the Supreme Audit Institution, and public and parliamentary scrutiny.

> ① **How and why to use?** The OECD Best Practices are short, clear and concise, while still covering a broad spectrum of good budget transparency practices as identified by OECD countries. Use the Best Practices for an accessible overview of the important issues, and to quickly identify the main "gaps" to be addressed. While some of the practices outlined are still relatively advanced, for the most modern guidance (e.g. on issues such as open data and medium-term budgeting), you should supplement the Best Practices by consulting also the other guidance materials.
>
> **Quick link:** http://oe.cd/FL

> **OECD Recommendation on Budgetary Governance (2015)**: Budgetary governance covers the processes, laws, institutions and structures in place for formulating and delivering the budget, overseeing its implementation and ensuring its alignment with public goals. The OECD Recommendation of the Council on Budgetary Governance sets out **ten Budget Principles** (see below), presenting an overview of how various aspects of modern budgeting - including fiscal rules, performance budgeting, medium-term frameworks, parliaments and other institutions - should inter-connect to form a coherent and effective system. The Principles "embody and update" many elements of the earlier Best Practices, including by introducing a principle of participative and inclusive budgetary debate.

The OECD's 10 Budget Principles

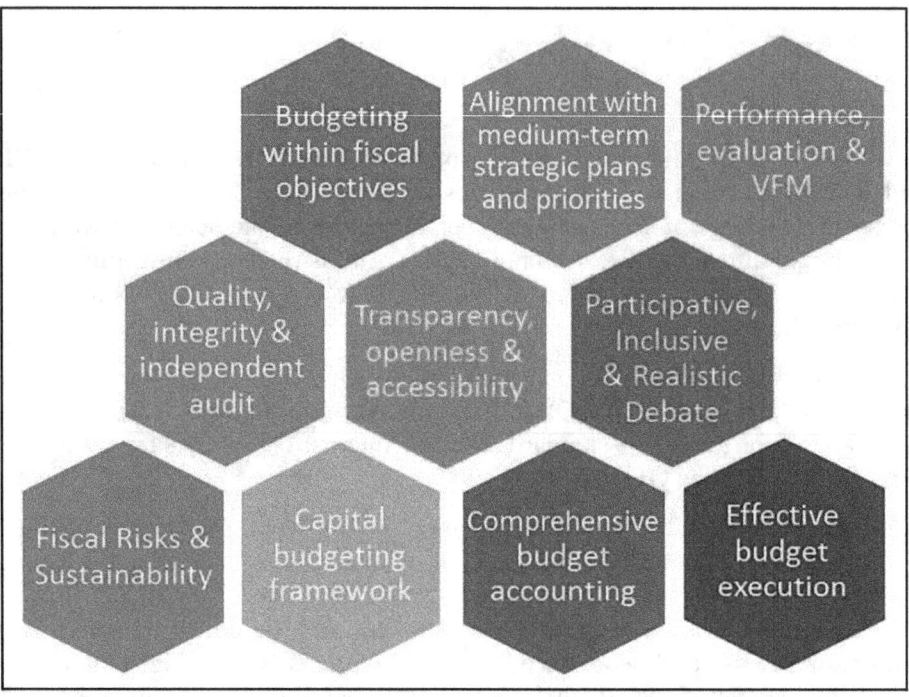

① **How and why to use?** As a formal OECD legal instrument, OECD member countries must adhere to the *Recommendation on Budgetary Governance;* non-OECD countries may also adhere in order to demonstrate their commitment to meeting the Budget Principles. Use the Budget Principles to gain a qualitative, rounded view of the budgeting system and of how it connects with other pillars of modern public governance including integrity, open data, and forging links between budgeting and planning for strategic goals. The Principles are also designed to be of relevance also to budgeting at national, regional and municipal level. Countries may request **OECD Budget Reviews**, carried out using the budget principles, for peer discussion at the SBO and regional networks.

Quick link: http://oe.cd/UA

See also:

- OECD Principles for Independent Fiscal Institutions (2014): Official guidance on the design and governance of independent fiscal councils and parliamentary budget offices. **Quick link:** http://oe.cd/FN

- OECD Principles for Public Governance of Public-Private Partnerships (2012): Official guidance on how governments can get value-for-money and manage risk in the design and delivery of PPP-funded projects. **Quick link:** http://oe.cd/1xT

- OECD Recommendation on Digital Government Strategies (2014): Official guidance on using digital government approaches, including open data, to promote citizen-driven public policy. **Quick link:** http://oe.cd/DigGovRev

- OECD Recommendation on Public Procurement (2015): Official guidance on using public procurement as a strategic tool for achieving efficiency and advancing public policy objectives. **Quick link:** http://oe.cd/W7

Public Expenditure and Financial Accountability (PEFA)

PEFA began in 2001 as a means to harmonise assessment of public financial management (PFM) across the development partner organisations. It was created through a joint initiative by seven international development partners: The European Commission, International Monetary Fund, World Bank, and the governments of France, Norway, Switzerland, and the United Kingdom.

PEFA was created to provide a standard methodology and reference tool for PFM diagnostic assessments. PEFA was also intended to provide a basis for dialogue on PFM reform strategies and priorities and a pool of information that could contribute more broadly to research and analysis of PFM. Since 2001 PEFA has become the acknowledged standard for PFM assessments. More than 540 PFM assessment reports from 150 countries at national and subnational levels have been completed as of October 1, 2016.

How does PEFA work?

PEFA assesses the strengths and weaknesses of PFM using quantitative indicators based on international good practice to measure performance. PEFA is designed to provide a snapshot of PFM performance at specific points in time using a methodology that can be replicated in successive assessments, giving a summary of changes over time. The PEFA framework includes a report that provides an overview of the PFM system and evidence-based measurement against 31 performance indicators. It also provides an assessment of the implications for overall system performance and desirable public financial management outcomes. It provides a foundation for reform planning, dialogue on strategy and priorities, and progress monitoring.

PEFA is a tool that helps governments achieve sustainable improvements in PFM practices within an integrated, evidence-based assessment across seven pillars of PFM.

The 7 pillars of PFM performance

PEFA reports outline the economic environment faced by the public sector, examine the nature of policy-based strategy and planning, and analyse how budget decisions are implemented. They assess the implications of strengths and weaknesses in PFM for aggregate fiscal discipline, strategic allocation of resources and efficiency of service delivery.

PEFA examines the controls used by governments to ensure that resources are obtained and used as intended. It emphasises transparency and accountability in terms of access to information, reporting and audit, and dialogue on PFM policies and actions. PEFA considers the institutions, laws, regulations, internal control and standards used by governments in the PFM process. It also examines the results arising from the operation of PFM in key areas such as budget outturns, effectiveness of controls, timeliness of reporting, and implementation of audit findings and recommendations.

> ① **How and why to use?** Governments use PEFA to obtain a snapshot of their own PFM performance. PEFA offers a common basis for examining PFM performance across national and subnational governments. In addition to governments, the other users of PEFA include civil society organisations and international development institutions. PEFA scores and reports allow all users of the information to gain a quick overview of the strengths and weaknesses of a country's PFM system. Users also see the implications of the overall performance results for the key goals of fiscal discipline, strategic resource allocation, and efficient service delivery and for the seven pillars across the breadth of PFM activities.
>
> The PEFA analysis contributes to dialogue on the need and priorities for PFM reform. It provides momentum for PFM reform and acts as a catalyst for action. It helps governments to identify areas for further analysis and review. It fosters stakeholder co-ordination around a common, well accepted assessment framework.
>
> Most countries that have used PEFA have applied it successively every few years to monitor progress over time and to help refocus and rejuvenate their PFM reform agenda.

What else does PEFA offer?

In addition to the methodology and reports, the programme provides guidance for analysis and reporting. The programme provides support, monitoring, and analysis of PEFA assessments. The PEFA Secretariat offers free advice on the use of PEFA as one of many sources of information for examining and improving PFM performance. Detailed guidance for governments, project managers, assessors, and users of PEFA reports is available from the PEFA website: www.pefa.org. The website also provides information on more than 540 PEFA reports, and is constantly updated. It allows access to performance scores and other data from all published reports and is a repository for PEFA-related research.

World Bank Group

Like the IMF, the **World Bank Group** was also established in 1944 as part of the Bretton Woods Agreement. Its mission is to alleviate poverty and promote development around the world through making available financial assistance and providing advice and aid on good governance. The World Bank is committed to promoting fiscal transparency at the global and national levels, recognising its contribution to macroeconomic stability, greater efficiency and equity in fiscal policies and increased public trust in government.

Through a number of programmes and projects, the World Bank has leveraged international platforms and initiatives to support client governments design and implement fiscal transparency reforms and improve fiscal governance. It has also worked closely with partner institutions to surface and disseminate international good practices with the objective of helping countries better achieve transparency dividends.

How does the World Bank promote fiscal transparency?

Public Expenditure and Financial Accountability (PEFA) Framework – The World Bank is one of the key institutional partners of the PEFA framework. One of the International Development Association (IDA) 18 recommendations/proposed actions under the Governance and Institutions pillar is to support at least 10 IDA countries in performing 2nd or subsequent PEFA assessments, as part of the broader objective of improving public expenditure, financial management, and procurement.

BOOST - Boost promotes the effective use of budget data for improved budgetary decision-making, analysis, transparency, and accountability. The programme strives to make well-classified and highly disaggregated budget data available for policymakers and practitioners within government, researchers, and civil society. The programme assists client governments clean, verify, organise, and disseminate their entire public spending datasets in machine-readable, easily accessible formats. It facilitates the dissemination of country BOOST datasets via *i)* the World Bank's Open Budgets Portal, a one stop shop for budget microdata worldwide, and *ii)* through the development of country-owned web portals. The programme also trains non-state actors, such as CSO representatives and journalists, on how to effectively access and use budget data to improve the policy dialogue around public expenditure.

Open Contracting - The Open Contracting programme supports client government adoption of norms, practices, and methodologies for increased disclosure and participation in public contracting. This involves the disclosure of relevant public contracting information, from planning through contract award and implementation, in order to allow for effective monitoring and accountability of how governments are spending taxpayers' money.

OpenGov Global Solutions Group (GSG) - The OpenGov GSG has as its objective the enhanced co-ordination of the World Bank's efforts around open government reforms, which include fiscal transparency practices around disclosure, coverage, content, accessibility, and reusability. This serves to ensure that the World Bank plays a leadership role in defining the growing global agenda around open government initiatives and better addresses growing client demand for such work. It also promotes the research, design, implementation, and evaluation of open government reforms.

Public Expenditure Reviews (PER) - PERs analyse both the level and pattern of a country's public expenditure in order to assess the effectiveness and equity of public spending, as well as to identify bottlenecks and other issues preventing greater spending effectiveness. These annually published World Bank reports are available to the public and are overseen by a wide range of stakeholders, including representatives from civil society.

Financial Management Information System (FMIS) - Open Budget Data survey - This detailed assessment analyses the ways in which FMIS can be used not only for government accounting and budget control, but also to publish reliable open budget data and promote transparency. It identifies indicators around existence, source/reliability, scope, and content to assess the web publishing platforms.

GIFT Stewardship, OGP, and OGP Fiscal Openness Working Group (FOWG) - As a founding lead steward of GIFT, the World Bank is responsible for helping lead the network and working closely with GIFT's Network Director and Coordination Team. The World Bank collaborates with GIFT in supporting fiscal transparency through the OGP's FOWG. Additionally, one of the Governance and Institutions recommendations/proposed actions in IDA18 is to support at least one-third of IDA countries to operationalise reform commitments toward the OGP agenda - including fiscal transparency commitments - in order to strengthen transparent, accountable, participatory, and inclusive governments.

Other relevant organisations and standards

In addition to the above organisations which deal with the broad aspects of budget transparency, there are some other professional and advocacy organisations that promote the benefits of transparency in their areas.

The **Extractive Industries Transparency Initiative (EITI)** was founded in 2003 to promote integrity in the management of revenues from extractive industries (oil, gas, metals, mineral endowments etc.) as this sector has been vulnerable to systematic corruption in many countries. The EITI standard promotes full transparency regarding all financial flows connected with resource extraction.
www.eiti.org

INTOSAI is the International Organisation of Supreme Audit Institutions (national external audit bodies for government accounts). Founded in 1953, it now has 194 full members and 5 associate members, and it promotes knowledge sharing and standard-setting among the global SAI community. The International Standards of Supreme Audit Institutions (ISSAI) are the professional standards and best practice guidelines promulgated by INTOSAI.
www.intosai.org

Transparency International was founded in 1993 to advocate strong and effective anti-corruption practices around the world. Its areas of focus include development of international conventions and norms; highlighting the systematic misappropriation of national wealth by those in leadership; ensuring that elections are held fairly and openly in line with democratic standards; and ensuring that global companies can be held accountable for their actions at home and in other countries.
www.transparency.org

Chapter 2

Applying budget transparency in different areas: OECD guidance on topics and resources

> *For different institutions or sectors, different standards or guidelines on budget transparency will be of most interest. This chapter allows users to navigate directly to the transparency-related resources available across five key dimensions of (i) government or executive branch (ii) parliament or legislature (iii) independent public institutions, including audit offices and fiscal councils (iv) citizens and civil society organisations and (v) the private sector, including its role in infrastructure and in managing natural resource endowments.*

Navigating the international standards and guidance

Chapter 2 of the Toolkit uses "signposts" to point you to the established international standards and to additional resources. The table below serves as a key to the abbreviations used.

Core international standards and reference frameworks on budget and fiscal transparency

Official standards / legal instruments	
IMF Code	IMF (2014), *The Fiscal Transparency Code*
OECD Budget Principles	OECD (2015) *Recommendation of the Council on Budgetary Governance*
Other Core reference materials	
GIFT High Level Principles	GIFT (2012), *High-Level Principles on Fiscal Transparency, Participation, and Accountability*
IBP Open Budget Survey	IBP (2017), *Guide to the Open Budget Questionnaire*
OECD Best Practices	OECD (2002), *Best Practices for Budget Transparency*
PEFA	PEFA (2016), *Framework for assessing public financial management*
Other key international guidance, tools and professional / technical standards	
CPA Benchmarks	Commonwealth Parliamentary Association (2015), Recommended Benchmarks for Democratic Legislatures
EITI	EITI (2016), The EITI Standard 2016
GIFT Public Participation	GIFT (2015), Principles of Public Participation in Fiscal Policy
G20 Open Data	G20 (2015), G20 anti-corruption Open Data Principles
IMF GFSM	IMF (2014), Government Finance Statistics Manual
IPSAS	IPSASB (2016), International Public Sector Accounting Standards
ISSAI	International Organisation of Supreme Audit Institutions, The International Standards of Supreme Audit Institutions
Open Data Charter	International Open Data Charter http://opendatacharter.net/
OECD Digital Government	OECD (2014), Recommendation of the Council on Digital Government Strategies
OECD IFI Principles	OECD (2014) Recommendation of the Council on Principles for Independent Fiscal Institutions
OECD Public Procurement	OECD (2015), OECD Recommendation of the Council on Public Procurement

Multi-dimensional map of Budget Transparency

This Chapter of the Toolkit on Budget Transparency presents alternative ways of finding the budget and fiscal transparency materials of interest to users in particular areas, based on the "multi-dimensional map of budget transparency".

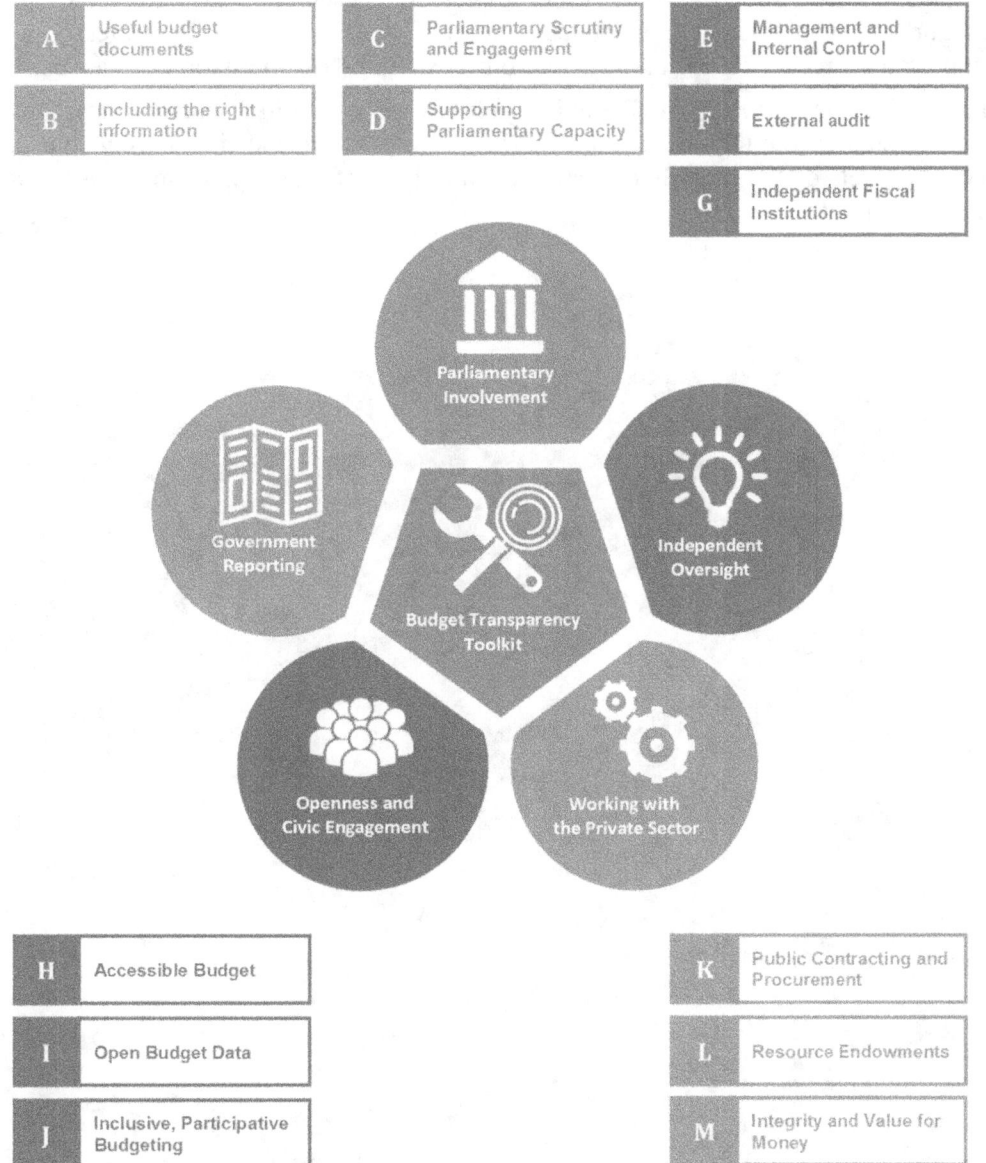

As you can see from the figure above, a five-fold presentation of budget transparency information is used:

1. The executive branch of government
2. The parliament or legislative branch
3. Independent oversight institutions
4. Citizens and civil society
5. Private sector engagement.

Under each of these dimensions, key topics are presented, drawn from the various international standards and guidance materials, and the specific references are "signposted" directly below, along with some examples of international practice. Each topic also includes **suggested starting points** which are initial, illustrative orientation aids suggested by the OECD. Naturally, these points are intended to introduce users to selected aspects of the underlying materials, and are not a substitute for consulting the official standards.

 ## Clear budget information from government

The public should be presented with high quality financial and non-financial information on past, present, and forecast fiscal activities, performance, fiscal risks, and public assets and liabilities.

- GIFT High-level Principles on Fiscal Transparency

Fiscal reports should provide a comprehensive, relevant, timely, and reliable overview of the government's financial position and performance. Budgets and their underlying fiscal forecasts should provide a clear statement of the government's budgetary objectives and policy intentions, and comprehensive, timely, and credible projections of the evolution of the public finances.

- IMF Code on Fiscal Transparency

Ensure that budget documents and data are open, transparent and accessible through the availability of clear, factual budget reports which should inform the key stages of policy formulation, consideration and debate, as well as implementation and review.

- OECD Recommendation on Budgetary Governance

	In this section
A	Providing useful budget-related documents during the annual cycle
B	Including the right financial information in budget-related documents

| A | **Providing useful budget-related documents during the annual cycle** |

Official documents should provide a useful overview of the fiscal activities of the public sector in a regular and timely manner, to inform better scrutiny and decision-making throughout the budget cycle. The main budget-related documents are described in this section. Such reports should also be open and accessible, including through the use of digital technologies, as outlined in *Openness and civic engagement* section, and should include a level of detail (whether specific or aggregate-level) appropriate to the stage of the budget cycle. While the most important elements of such documents are covered in more detail in section B, some of the key features and functions of these reports are outlined in this section.

A.1 The pre-budget statement sets out the budget strategy, by introducing the government's high-level budget plans for the forthcoming fiscal year. By promoting awareness and debate on the budget aggregates, the implications of maintaining existing policies, and interactions with the broader economy, it sets expectations for the budget and paves the way for an informed scrutiny of the actual budget.

▻ **Suggested starting points** are that the pre-budget report should:

- be published at least one month before the executive's **budget proposal** is tabled
- state the government's broad fiscal policy intentions for the budget, as well as …
- … macroeconomic assumptions and forecast levels of revenue, expenditure and fiscal balance and public debt.

🌐 Examples from around the world	✛ International Standards and Guidance	
France: The Preparatory Budget Report (*Rapport préparatoire au débat d'orientation budgétaire, DOFP*) is presented to the parliament before June 30th each year. It is an important milestone prior to the submission of the Budget Bill to the parliament later in the fiscal year. The DOFP announces to the parliament the main changes to the government's economic and fiscal policies, expected path of the State's finances for the next fiscal year and sets provisional ceilings on public expenditure.	OECD Budget Principles	4
	IBP Open Budget Survey	Q54-58
	OECD Budget Principles	1.2
	PEFA	PI-5, 9, 14-17

A.2 The executive's **budget proposal (or draft budget)** is a comprehensive document (or set of documents) that specifies the government's plans for the forthcoming year, and is submitted by the government to parliament for approval. The budget is a key instrument of public policy, and so it is appropriate that this document is clear and accessible, and that it receive thorough, meaningful scrutiny by public and parliament.

⮕ **Suggested starting points** are that the budget proposal should:

- be submitted in good time to allow for proper review by parliament (see **C.3**)
- show the government's objectives for fiscal policy, and priorities for expenditure and revenue policy, in the year ahead and over the medium term
- use internationally-recognised standards of revenues and expenditures
- describe the cost and assessed impact of all new policy measures (see also **J.2**).

🌐 Examples from around the world	International Standards and Guidance	
Iceland: Regulations provide that the executive's budget proposal must be submitted to the Legislature more than three months before the beginning of the fiscal year, until the second Tuesday of September.	IMF Code	1.3.1, 2.1.3, 2.2.2, 2.3.1
	OECD Budget Principles	4
Tunisia: The Finance Organic Law provides that the executive's annual Finance Act (FA) shall include the annual financial forecasts, appropriate money for public policies, and includes a series of legal provisions such as new taxes, changes in entitlement programmes, or general provisions for exerting fiscal discipline over ministries and other public bodies. It shall also link the annual financial forecasts to the Economic and Social Development Plan and the budget.	IBP Open Budget Survey	Q 1-52
	OECD Best Practices	1.1
	PEFA	PI-4, 5, 8, 9, 14-17

A.3 The approved budget is the budget as formally adopted by parliament, and is the definitive point of reference for the raising of revenues and allocating, and accounting for, public funds. Most countries recognise, in their laws and/or constitutions, the importance of the approved budget in creating a legal basis for levying of taxes and the allocation of public funds.

▷ **Suggested starting points** are that the approved budget should:

- be published as soon as it is approved by the legislature
- have legal effect before the start of the budget year
- include the same level of detail as the executive's **budget proposal** to help in identifying all significant deviations from it.

🌐 Examples from around the world	International Standards and Guidance	
United Kingdom: The annual budget is presented to the House of Commons by the Chancellor of the Exchequer, and is debated for several days. Tax-raising "Ways and Means Resolutions" must be approved by the House, and all budget-related tax measures are subsequently included in a Finance Bill which is passed like any other legislation. Expenditure measures are authorised initially by "Supply Resolutions", which give only provisional authorisation for expenditure and are then followed by the Supply & Appropriation Bill.	IMF Code	2.2.2
	OECD Budget Principles	4
	IBP Open Budget Survey	Q 59-63
	OECD Best Practices	1.1
	PEFA	PI-9, 17, 18

A.4 The supplementary budget contains proposed amendments to the main annual budget. Such a mechanism should be used to authorise significant additions or changed allocations which were not foreseen at the time of the original budget and appropriations.

☞ **Suggested starting points** are that the supplementary budget should:

- put forward all proposed amendments at the same time
- include an explanation of the basis for the supplementary budget measures
- show the effect (if any) on fiscal policy objectives
- be authorised by the parliament prior to the expenditures being incurred.

🌎 Examples from around the world	✣ International Standards and Guidance	
Sweden: The Government can revise the central government budget by proposing an increase to an agency's budget for unanticipated needs in connection with the Spring Fiscal Policy Bill and the Budget Bill in September. Revised budget increases are usually offset by reducing budgets for other agencies by a corresponding amount or by borrowing from next year's appropriation. In Sweden, supplementary budgets are relatively small and are typically used for technical adjustments rather than new policy.	IMF Code	2.4.2
	OECD Budget Principles	5, 7
	IBP Open Budget Survey	Q 115-117
	PEFA	PI-1, 2, 3, 15, 18, 21

A.5 Pre-execution budget profiles or cash-flow forecasts show how budget expenditures and revenues are projected to arise over the course of the year in broad terms, and provide a useful benchmark for in-year monitoring. Preparing useful budget profiles or cash-flow forecasts requires careful attention to seasonal factors, expected once-off events and other factors that can lead to large fluctuations in revenues and expenditures.

Suggested starting points are that these budget profiles or forecasts should:

- be published close to, or ideally before, the start of the budget year
- allow for early identification of budgetary overruns /underspends and other risks.

Examples from around the world	International Standards and Guidance	
Ireland: The Department of Finance publishes monthly profiles of expenditures and revenues at the start of each year and these profiles form an important point of reference for monthly reporting to the public on budgeting execution.	OECD Budget Principles	7
	OECD Best Practices	1.3
	PEFA	PI-21

A.6 In-year budget execution reports provide a snapshot of the budget's implementation during the budget year, and signal to the government (and to the public) the need to take corrective action where appropriate.

☞ **Suggested starting points** are that the budget execution reports should:

- be published quarterly or (ideally) monthly, shortly after the end of each period
- include a short commentary to assist in interpreting the report, especially explanations of any significant divergences from the corresponding budget profiles.

🌐 Examples from around the world	International Standards and Guidance	
United States: Monthly budget execution reports show monthly obligations reported by agencies. Two versions are prepared and available, one showing a breakdown by agency and bureau, the other one sorting information by appropriations sub-committee. Additional to the information referring to the previous month, the reports show cumulative obligations for previous quarters of the fiscal year and historical obligations reported in the previous fiscal year when available.	IMF Code	1.2.1, 1.3.1, 1.4.31
	OECD Budget Principles	7
	IBP Open Budget Survey	Q 68-75
	OECD Best Practices	1.3
	PEFA	PI-28

A.7 **The mid-year implementation report** is an analysis of the budget's effects provided about halfway through the budget year and provides a comprehensive update on the implementation of the budget. In addition to its use for budget oversight, the mid-year report can also yield useful insights which can inform the pre-budget deliberations for the following year.

Suggested starting points are that the mid-year implementation report should:

- be published within six weeks of mid-year
- include an updated forecast of the budget outcomes for the budget year
- report on the expected budget impact of any revisions to economic assumptions, and of any government policy decisions that may have been taken earlier that year.

🌐 Examples from around the world	International Standards and Guidance	
Sri Lanka: The mid-year implementation report (Mid-Year Fiscal Position Report) is required by its Fiscal Management Act to present an evaluation against the government's fiscal strategy. The report is required to be placed in parliament within two weeks from its date of release. It reviews the performance of government revenue, expenditures, cash-flow operations and borrowings for the first four months of the relevant year. The report also provides updated information relating to macroeconomic performance, government debt, balance of payments and credit.	OECD Budget Principles	7
	IBP Open Budget Survey	Q 76-83
	OECD Best Practices	1.4
	PEFA	PI-9, 27

A.8 Year-end reporting is essential for accountability, both for reporting on actual budget execution during the year (budget execution reports) and for illustrating the situation of the government's accounts at the end of the fiscal year (financial statements). These reports are normally submitted for audit by the Supreme Audit Institution (see **F.2**).

☞ **Suggested starting points** are that year-end reporting should:

- be released within six months of the end of the fiscal year
- be presented in a way that corresponds with the format of the approved budget
- ideally, present financial statements on an accrual basis.

🌐 Examples from around the world	International Standards and Guidance	
United Kingdom: In the year-end report, the government undertakes a more detailed evaluation of an individual ministry's spending programme (Spending Review) including assessing what the government spent over the last few years in terms of trends, productivity and value.	IMF Code	1.1.2, 1.1.3, 1.2.2, 1.4.2, 1.4.3
	OECD Budget Principles	7
	IBP Open Budget Survey	Q 84-96
	OECD Best Practices	1.5
	PEFA	PI-6, 10, 29
	IPSAS	

A.9 **The long-term report** assesses the long-term sustainability of public finances and government policies. The report shows the projections of the evolution of the public finances over the long term, particularly in light of projected demographic changes and (for some countries) the continued availability of natural resource endowments such as oil, natural gas or mineral ores. In addition to long-term sustainability, this report can also contribute to national debate on the issue of inter-generational equity - i.e. how the burden of taxation and the enjoyment of benefits, are over a long time period across multiple generations.

Suggested starting points are that the long-term report should:

- be produced at least every three to five years
- use internationally-comparable indicators of long-term sustainability
- ideally, suggest near-term (2-5 years) as well as longer-term policy messages.

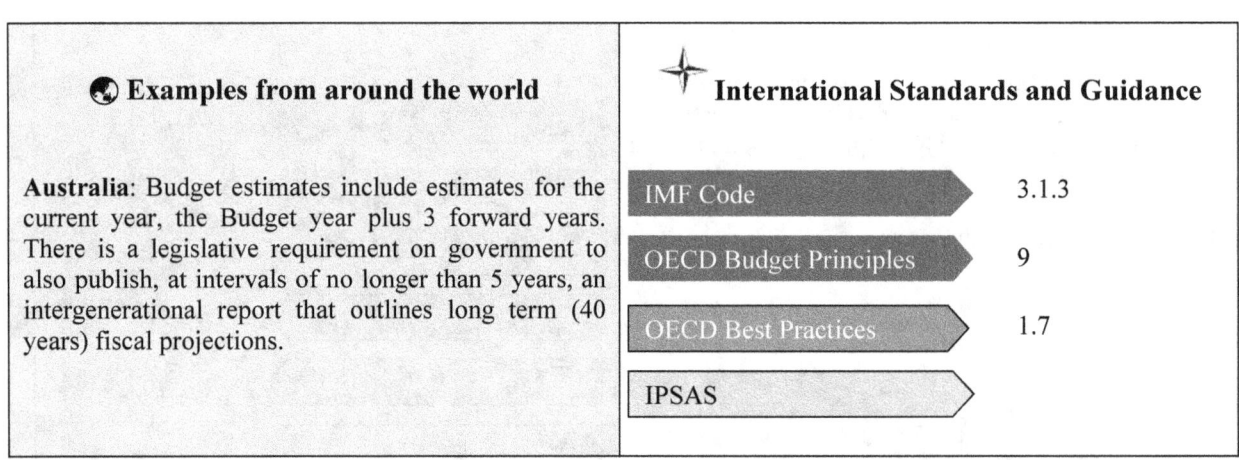

Examples from around the world	International Standards and Guidance	
Australia: Budget estimates include estimates for the current year, the Budget year plus 3 forward years. There is a legislative requirement on government to also publish, at intervals of no longer than 5 years, an intergenerational report that outlines long term (40 years) fiscal projections.	IMF Code	3.1.3
	OECD Budget Principles	9
	OECD Best Practices	1.7
	IPSAS	

A.10 Reporting on fiscal risk provides an overall assessment of the range and scale of factors which have the potential to blow the public finances off course. Such reporting, if integrated alongside the annual economic and fiscal documentation, can provide a good sense of how robust and resilient the public finances are, thus informing the national debate about the appropriate budgetary strategy and whether there are sufficient safety mechanisms in place.

Suggested starting points are that reporting on fiscal risk should:

- accompany the economic and fiscal documentation each year
- outline the government strategies to manage and mitigate various types of risk
- to the extent possible, provide an indicative quantification or measure of fiscal risks
- ideally, be presented in a single, comprehensive annual fiscal risk report.

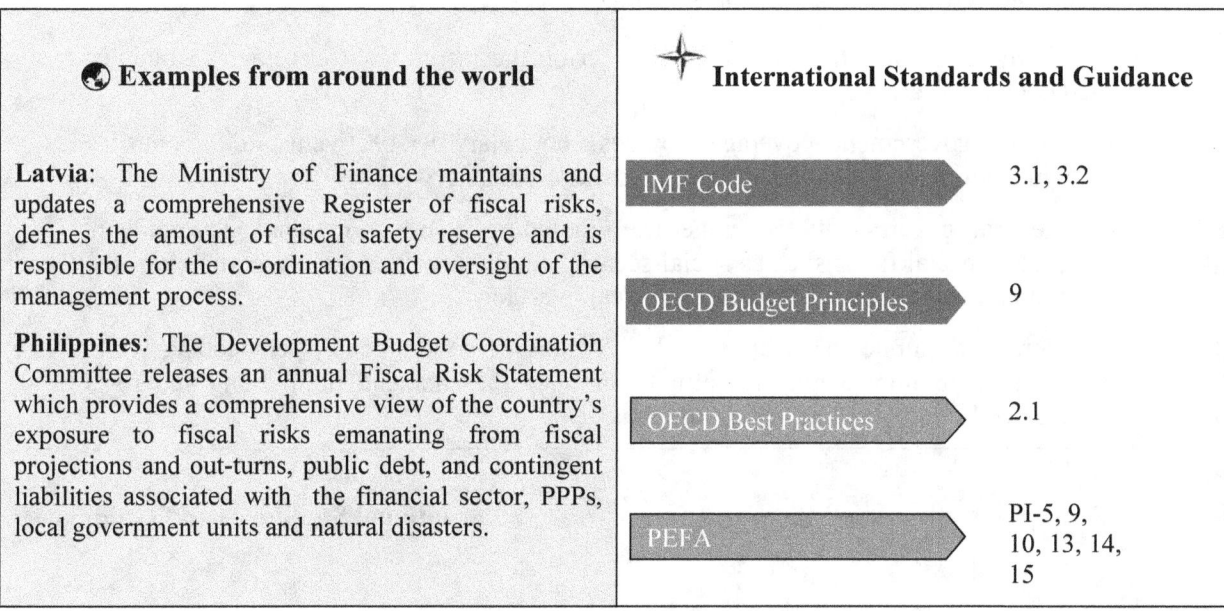

🌐 **Examples from around the world**

Latvia: The Ministry of Finance maintains and updates a comprehensive Register of fiscal risks, defines the amount of fiscal safety reserve and is responsible for the co-ordination and oversight of the management process.

Philippines: The Development Budget Coordination Committee releases an annual Fiscal Risk Statement which provides a comprehensive view of the country's exposure to fiscal risks emanating from fiscal projections and out-turns, public debt, and contingent liabilities associated with the financial sector, PPPs, local government units and natural disasters.

International Standards and Guidance

IMF Code	3.1, 3.2
OECD Budget Principles	9
OECD Best Practices	2.1
PEFA	PI-5, 9, 10, 13, 14, 15

B	Including the right financial information in budget-related documents

The quality and comprehensiveness of financial information contained in the various budget-related documents are essential for transparency, accountability and good governance. While the various budgetary reports fulfil a range of different functions, taken as a whole the documents should provide insights into the various factors that are relevant for budgetary decision making.

B.1 Institutional coverage – The annual authorisation of expenditure by the parliament is provided for a limited range of bodies (the "budgetary entities", including central government ministries, departments, specialised boards, commissions or agencies). Government may in addition report the financial position and performance of the central government, general government or public sector as a whole in the budget documentation and/or year-end financial reporting (see **A.8**). A wide institutional coverage provides a more complete picture of the country's overall fiscal position, facilitates comprehensive analysis of public finances, and reduces the incentives for governments to use some entities for off-budget fiscal activity.

⚑ **Suggested starting points** in considering the institutional coverage of budget-related documents are:

- "central government" coverage provides a budgetary perspective useful to countries with significant executive agencies and extra-budgetary funds

- "general government" coverage (i.e. including also sub-national governments and/or special funds such as social security funds) provides a more comprehensive and internationally-comparable statistical overview

- a broader "public sector" (also called "whole of government") perspective, while complex to implement, is useful to monitor the financial obligations and risks created by state-controlled corporations.

🌐 **Examples from around the world**

European Union: Member states of the EU present their public finances on a "general government" basis for the purposes of multi-lateral surveillance under the Stability and Growth Pact, even where they may use different approaches for purely national purposes. This allows for comparison of public deficit and debt figures on a cross-country basis, even though the various countries have very different unitary, federal and confederal budget systems.

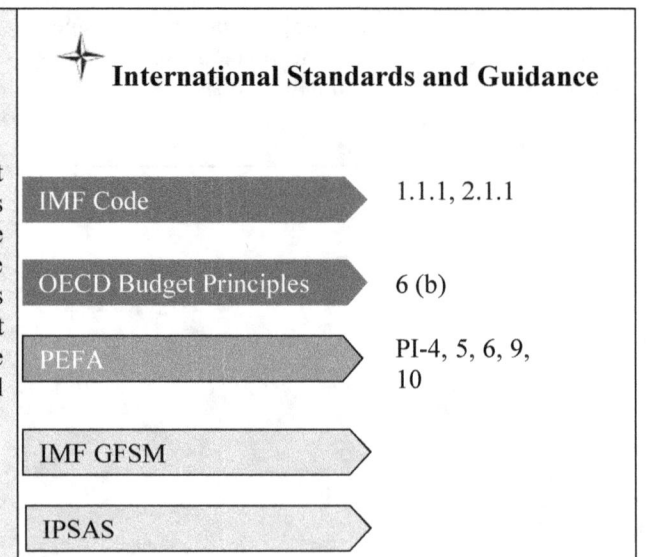

International Standards and Guidance

IMF Code	1.1.1, 2.1.1
OECD Budget Principles	6 (b)
PEFA	PI-4, 5, 6, 9, 10
IMF GFSM	
IPSAS	

B.2 The **quality, reliability and comparability** of budget information are crucial, if the documents are to provide a sound basis for decision-making, scrutiny and accountability. There is extensive international guidance and standardisation of rules and procedures dealing with these matters.

Suggested starting points are that the budget information should:

- use consistent accounting policies for all documents, explaining any changes
- be consistent also in format from year to year, and from report to report
- use international standards for financial and fiscal statistics
- be subject to internal controls (see section **E**) and independent audit (section **F**).

Examples from around the world	International Standards and Guidance	
Australia: The Final Budget Outcome is the government's key ex post accountability document and is published within 3 months of year-end, using the same basis as the budget and the mid-year update, both as regards flows (revues, expenditures and balances) and stocks (net debt and net financial worth). All fiscal information is based on common reporting standards largely in line with SFSM 2011 standards, with any departures from these standards clearly explained.	IMF Code	1.3, 1.4
	OECD Budget Principles	6.10 (c)-(e)
	OECD Best Practices	3.1-3.3
	PEFA	PI-4, 26, 29, 30

B.3 Comprehensiveness of information – Budget-related documents should show the full range of information relevant for fiscal decision-making and accountability. Again, there are extensive international standards and guidance materials in this area.

☞ **Suggested starting points** are that the budget-related documents should:

- show all key economic assumptions, as well as sensitivity analyses
- account for all expenditures and revenues, including those of extra-budgetary funds
- include information on tax expenditures
- present a balance sheet of assets and liabilities, financial and (ideally) non-financial
- present a medium-term (3-5 year) perspective on budgetary forecasts and plans.

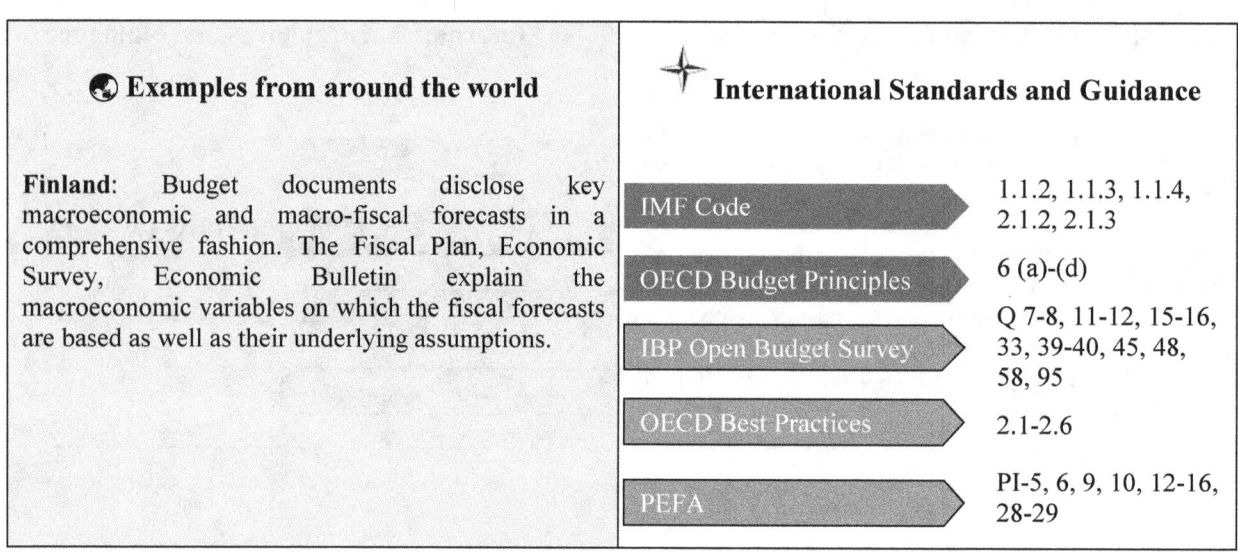

🌐 **Examples from around the world**

Finland: Budget documents disclose key macroeconomic and macro-fiscal forecasts in a comprehensive fashion. The Fiscal Plan, Economic Survey, Economic Bulletin explain the macroeconomic variables on which the fiscal forecasts are based as well as their underlying assumptions.

International Standards and Guidance

IMF Code	1.1.2, 1.1.3, 1.1.4, 2.1.2, 2.1.3
OECD Budget Principles	6 (a)-(d)
IBP Open Budget Survey	Q 7-8, 11-12, 15-16, 33, 39-40, 45, 48, 58, 95
OECD Best Practices	2.1-2.6
PEFA	PI-5, 6, 9, 10, 12-16, 28-29

B.4 Policy relevance of budget information – Budget documents should be clear and transparent in showing how financial allocations are aligned with, and supportive of, the policy priorities of government. As the budget is an important tool of overall public policy, such information is useful for parliamentarians and for the wider public in holding the government to account for budgetary choices.

▷ **Suggested starting points** are that the budget information should:

- show performance information (e.g. outputs, targets, results) for key policy areas
- use a standard format for performance reporting, across different policy areas
- show linkages with higher-level strategic and outcome goals of government
- show the impacts of budget decisions on different groups and sectors (see **J.2**).

🌎 Examples from around the world	International Standards and Guidance	
Austria: Each policy area (programme) in the budget shows between 3 and 5 performance targets, at least one of which relates to gender.	IMF Code	2.3
	OECD Budget Principles	4(d), 8
United States: Each Federal Agency produces a variety of performance goals and objectives: Some of these are classed as Agency Priority Goals, which are a key focus of leadership action and accountability. See www.performance.gov	IBP Open Budget Survey	Q36, 47-52, 92-94
	OECD Best Practices	1.1
	PEFA	PI-8, 15, 16

Further guidance

> IFAC/CIPFA (2014), *International Framework: Good Governance in the Public Sector*, International Federation of Accountants / The Chartered Institute of Public Finance and Accountancy, www.ifac.org/publications-resources/international-framework-good-governance-public-sector
>
> IFAC (2015), *"Risk Management and Internal Control"*, International Federation of Accountants, www.ifac.org/publications-resources/bolt-built
>
> INTOSAI, ISSAI 100 (2013), *"Fundamental Principles of Public-Sector Auditing"*, the International Organisation of Supreme Audit Institutions, www.intosai.org/issai-executive-summaries/view/article/issai-100-fundamental-principles-of-public-sector-auditing.html
>
> INTOSAI, ISSAI 400 (2013), *"Fundamental Principles of Compliance Auditing"*, the International Organisation of Supreme Audit Institutions, www.intosai.org/issai-executive-summaries/view/article/issai-400-fundamental-principles-of-compliance-auditing.html
>
> IPSASB (2013), *International Public Sector Accounting Standards 32* (Service Concession Arrangements), International Public Sector Accounting Standard Board, www.ifac.org/system/files/publications/files/B8%20IPSAS_32.pdf
>
> IPSASB (2017), Recommended Practice Guideline 3, *Reporting on the Long-Term Sustainability of an Entity's Finances*, www.ifac.org/publications-resources/recommended-practice-guideline-3
>
> OECD (2013), *Brazil's Supreme Audit Institution: The Audit of the Consolidated Year-end Government Report*, OECD Publishing, Paris. http://dx.doi.org/10.1787/9789264188112-en

 **Parliamentary scrutiny and engagement**

The legislature should be provided with the authority, resources, and information required to effectively hold the executive to account for the use of public resources.

- GIFT High-Level Principles on Fiscal Transparency

The national parliament has a fundamental role in authorising budget decisions and in holding government to account. Countries should offer opportunities for the parliament and its committees to engage with the budget process at all key stages of the budget cycle, both ex ante *and* ex post *as appropriate.*

- OECD Recommendation on Budgetary Governance

Parliament should have the opportunity and the resources to effectively examine any fiscal report that it deems necessary.

- OECD Best Practices on Budget Transparency

In this section	
C	Benefiting from parliamentary engagement and scrutiny
D	Supporting parliamentary capacity

C	Benefiting from parliamentary engagement and scrutiny

Parliaments' "power of the purse" is a cornerstone of democratic governance. Parliaments play a formal role in scrutiny and authorisation of the executive's budget proposal and holding the executive to account, on behalf of citizens, for its decisions and for policy execution. In modern public governance, there are a range of opportunities where the budget cycle can benefit from the distinct democratic legitimacy of parliamentary input.

C.1 Parliamentary committees are a useful forum for focused, in-depth scrutiny and effective engagement with the budgetary process. Committee members build up specialised knowledge of budget-related topics, and the committees themselves can sustain an informed "accountability dialogue" with government ministries and agencies throughout the annual budget cycle, and from year to year. In addition to serving as key democratic forums in their own right, parliamentary committees may also benefit from inputs directly from citizens, civil society bodies and independent experts, who can contribute to an inclusive, informed parliamentary discussion on budget-related issues.

Suggested starting points are that parliamentary committees should:

- include sector-specific committees for detailed scrutiny in particular areas
- maintain a budget/finance committee to consider the executive's budget proposal
- maintain a finance/public accounts committee to engage with the issues raised in the reports of the Supreme Audit Institution including the year-end reporting
- provide for coherence and continuity of approach among the various committees
- consider allowing for structured, transparent inputs from citizens and civil society.

Examples from around the world

Germany: The Bundestag's Budget Committee has a strong and active role in scrutinising the government's draft budget. The committee sends "rapporteurs", along with representatives from the Supreme Audit Institution, into each ministry to discuss proposed spending allocations. This allows for a strong feedback loop from audit into the budget deliberations. The rapporteurs are responsible for this portfolio for the full electoral term, allowing them to develop expertise. The committee can propose amendments to the draft budget and place conditions on the execution of particular budget lines.

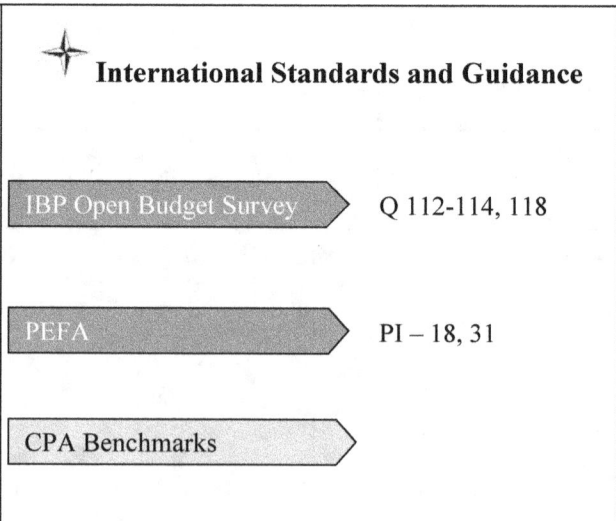

International Standards and Guidance

IBP Open Budget Survey — Q 112-114, 118

PEFA — PI – 18, 31

CPA Benchmarks

C.2 *Ex ante* parliamentary engagement allows parliamentarians' views on issues of fiscal and budgetary policy to inform the budget formulation process. In this way, the executive's budget proposal (A.2) can reflect the input and priorities of the legislature, which is particularly relevant for countries where the parliament lacks significant powers to amend the draft budget.

▷ **Suggested starting points** are that *ex ante* parliamentary engagement should:

- be informed by the government's **pre-budget statement (A.1)** on fiscal policy intentions and potential budgetary options
- be conducted in a realistic manner that takes account of overall fiscal constraints
- provide opportunities for public input through mechanisms such as public hearings, where national legal frameworks allow for this
- result in clear policy priorities and considerations from parliament to the executive.

🌐 Examples from around the world	International Standards and Guidance
Sweden: In Sweden the annual budget process is divided into two distinct phases, with a Spring Fiscal Policy Bill in April setting down broad aggregates for fiscal policy development, followed by a government Budget Bill in the autumn specifying allocations for the budget year ahead. The Spring Fiscal Policy Bill provides for parliamentary debate on fiscal policy in general terms. The main budgetary aggregates are voted on in a single spring vote.	OECD Budget Principles — 5(a), 5(b) IBP Open Budget Survey — Q 107, 136-138 PEFA — PI-17, 18

C.3 Parliamentary approval of the budget is a fundamental element of democratic accountability and oversight. Approval by the legislature confers democratic legitimacy on the levying of taxation and on the appropriation and use of public funds; at other phases of the budget cycle, the parliament can follow through on its accountability role based upon the approved budget allocations.

▷ **Suggested starting points** are that parliamentary approval should:

- be based on public parliamentary debate of the government's budget proposal
- allow enough time for the parliament to undertake in-depth scrutiny – three months is a useful benchmark, although the quality and depth of review are important
- ideally, take account of how the executive has responded to the policy priorities and considerations from the *ex ante* parliamentary engagement phase
- take place prior to the start of the fiscal year.

🌐 Examples from around the world	✦ International Standards and Guidance	
Denmark: The finance bill for the next fiscal year must be submitted to the Danish Parliament not later than four months before the beginning of that fiscal year (Article 45 of the Constitution). The finance bill has to be passed before the end of the calendar year.	IMF Code	2.2.1, 2.2.2, 2.4.2
	IBP Open Budget Survey	Q 108-111
	OECD Best Practices	1.1
	PEFA	PI – 17, 18
	CPA Benchmarks	7.2

C.4 Parliamentary scrutiny of budget execution and outturn ensures that public funds are being/have been used for the purposes intended, and that policies are achieving their intended results. Careful monitoring of budget execution helps to underpin public confidence and trust in the use of public funds, and to guard against corruption, mismanagement and waste.

☞ **Suggested starting points** are that parliamentary scrutiny in this area should:

- make use of regular in-year/mid-year reports (see **A.6** and **A.7** above)
- require new prior parliamentary approval of significant in-year budget reallocations
- review the external audit report (see **F.2**) and other reports provided by the Supreme Audit Institution and publish recommendations for action
- ensure that the issues raised during scrutiny inform the subsequent budgetary cycle.

🌐 Examples from around the world	✦ International Standards and Guidance	
Austria: The Austrian Parliament decides on financial resources and on results (outcomes and outputs) as a part of annual budget bill. The Parliament also assesses the performance reports of government, reflecting critically on performance information and using it to ensure a more strategic budget debate.	IMF Code	2.4.2
	IBP Open Budget Survey	Q 114-118, 139
	OECD Best Practices	3.3
	PEFA	PI - 30, 31
	CPA Benchmarks	7.2.3

D	Supporting parliamentary capacity

In order to undertake budget scrutiny and oversight effectively, parliaments need to be equipped to engage in a professional manner with the financial and policy-related issues that are presented during the budgetary cycle.

D.1 Specialist analytical and research resources, such as in-house research services and budget units within parliaments, can promote a more informed engagement between the legislature and the executive. This is particularly important in the budgetary area, since budget-related documents can be highly complex and detailed, and the parliament must rely on specialist support to fulfil its mandate in budget approval and accountability.

▷ **Suggested starting points** are that such analytical and research resources should:

- provide technical, expert and non-partisan analysis of budgetary reports
- have full, timely access to fiscal and budget-related information from the executive
- consider augmenting specialist capacity through establishing an independent, clearly-mandated Parliamentary Budget Office (PBO, see G.1).

🌐 Examples from around the world	✦ International Standards and Guidance
United Kingdom: The UK Parliament and some of the devolved regional legislatures have established in-house technical units to support budget scrutiny and enhance transparency. For example, the Scottish Parliament, helped by its Financial Scrutiny Unit (FSU), negotiated with the executive to speed up the provision of detailed budget information for all portfolios, in order to enable effective oversight. In addition to providing in-depth technical analysis of the budget figures, the FSU has worked to simplify presentation of budget information. **PBOs** have been established in several countries around the world, including Australia, Austria, Canada, Italy, Korea, and the United States.	GIFT High Level Principles — 8 IBP Open Budget Survey — Q 103 OECD IFI Principles — 1-22

D.2 Continuing Professional Development (CPD) of parliamentarians on budgetary matters recognises that scrutiny of overall public spending, taxation and asset and liability management is a complex, demanding task of professional public representatives. For staff of government ministries and agencies, who deal in-depth with the budget cycle and documents each year, the process is usually familiar. For parliamentarians who have a broader range of issues to address, and who may have less familiarity with the budget process, additional support is needed. Careful attention should be paid to equipping parliamentarians with the knowledge and skills they need to engage effectively with the budgetary documentation and to input their views to the overall process.

Suggested starting points are that budget-related CPD for parliamentarians should:

- include induction training for parliamentarians, committee members and chairs
- cover domestic and international aspects of budgetary scrutiny and oversight.

Examples from around the world	International Standards and Guidance
United States: Since 1972, the US House of Representatives leadership have offered a training programme for incoming US representatives hosted by the Harvard Institute of Politics at The Kennedy School. It provides intensive seminars on major public policy issues such as foreign policy, health care and the Federal budget, led by prominent scholars and practitioners representing viewpoints from across the political spectrum.	OECD Budget Principles 10 (a)

Further guidance

Anderson, B. (2009), "The changing role of parliament in the budget process", *OECD Journal on Budgeting*, Vol. 9/1. http://dx.doi.org/10.1787/budget-v9-art2-en

Inter-Parliamentary Union (2008), "*Evaluating parliament: A self-assessment toolkit for parliaments*", www.ipu.org/pdf/publications/self-e.pdf

L'Assemblée parlementaire de la Francophonie (2009), *La réalité démocratique des Parlements: Quels critères d'évaluation?* Texte adopté lors de la XXXVème Session de l'APF (Paris, juillet 2009)

McGee, D. (2002), *The Overseers: Public Accounts Committees and Public Spending*, Pluto Press, London.

McGee, D. (2007), *The Budget Process: A Parliamentary Imperative*, Pluto Press, London.

Posner, P. and Park Chung-Keun (2007), "Role of the Legislature in the Budget Process: Recent Trends and Innovations", *OECD Journal on Budgeting*, Vol. 7/3. http://dx.doi.org/10.1787/budget-v7-art15-en

Schick, A. (2002), "Can National Legislatures Regain an Effective Voice in Budget Policy?", *OECD Journal on Budgeting*, Vol. 1/3. http://dx.doi.org/10.1787/budget-v1-art15-en

Stapenhurst, R., R. Pelizzo, and K. Jacobs (2014), *Following the Money: Comparing Parliamentary Public Accounts Committees*, Pluto Press, London.

Stapenhurst, R. et al. (2008), *Legislative Oversight and Budgeting: A World Perspective*, The International Bank for Reconstruction and Development/The World Bank, https://openknowledge.worldbank.org/handle/10986/6547

von Trapp, L. and J. Jacques (2011), "*Committee Structures for Budget Approval and Oversight*", 3rd Annual Meeting of OECD Parliamentary Budget Officials, www.oecd.org/officialdocuments/publicdisplaydocumentpdf/?cote=GOV/PGC/SBO(2011)6&doclanguage=en

 ## Independent oversight and control

The Supreme Audit Institution should have statutory independence from the executive, and the mandate, access to information, and appropriate resources to audit and report publicly on the raising and commitment of public funds.

- GIFT High-Level Principles on Fiscal Transparency

Promote the integrity and quality of budgetary forecasts, fiscal plans and budgetary implementation through rigorous quality assurance including independent audit

- OECD Recommendation on Budgetary Governance

The credibility of national budgeting – including the professional objectivity of economic forecasting, adherence to fiscal rules, longer-term sustainability and handling of fiscal risks – may also be supported through independent fiscal institutions or other structured, institutional processes for allowing impartial scrutiny of, and input to, government budgeting

- OECD Recommendation on Budgetary Governance

In this section	
E	Management and internal control of public money
F	Supporting the role of the Supreme Audit Institution (SAI)
G	An effective role for Independent Fiscal Institutions (IFIs)

E	Management and internal control of public money

The government needs to command credibility and trust in how it raises and spends public funds, and in its dealings with the private sector. Clear standards for managing public money, and regular audits to ensure that these standards are being upheld, are the basic tools for maintaining integrity and public trust.

E.1 Standards and Procedures for Managing Public Money set out explicitly the standards of probity and personal responsibilities of all officials in the government charged with managing public funds.

☞ **Suggested starting points** are that the standards and procedures should:

- apply across all public entities and at all levels of government
- specify the distinct procedures and duties at various stages of public financial management, including revenue administration and collection, orders and payments, payment terms and control of outstanding balances
- be subject to internal audit (see **E.2**) and external audit (see **F**)
- be openly available for the general public as well as for all government suppliers.

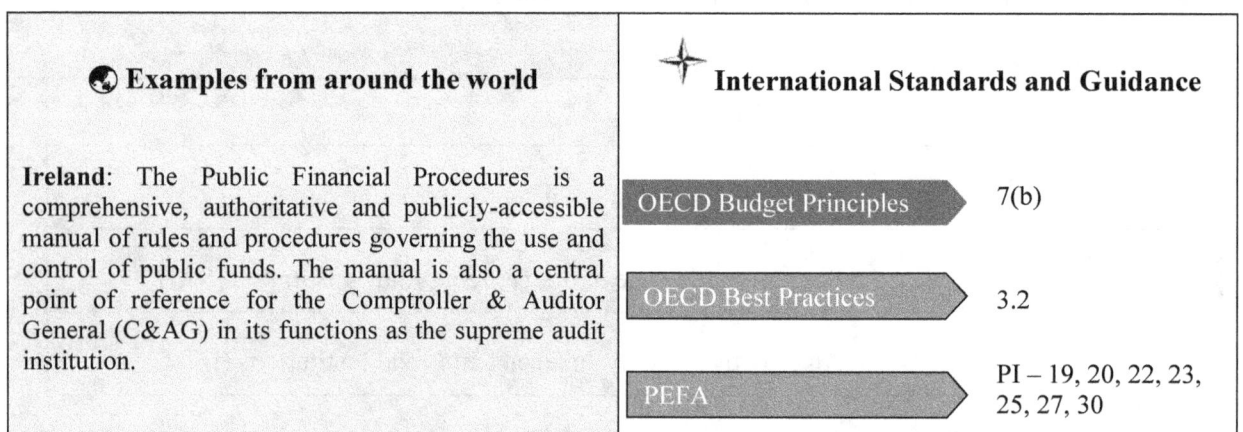

🌐 **Examples from around the world**

Ireland: The Public Financial Procedures is a comprehensive, authoritative and publicly-accessible manual of rules and procedures governing the use and control of public funds. The manual is also a central point of reference for the Comptroller & Auditor General (C&AG) in its functions as the supreme audit institution.

✦ **International Standards and Guidance**

OECD Budget Principles	7(b)
OECD Best Practices	3.2
PEFA	PI – 19, 20, 22, 23, 25, 27, 30

E.2 Internal audit procedures are essential for guarding public funds from misuse, fraud and waste. Financial inspectors and internal auditors also play an important role in helping to improve overall levels of organisational effectiveness.

▷ **Suggested starting points** are that internal audit procedures should:

- operate independently, in line with professional audit standards
- undertake regular audits of the main financial processes and main spending and revenue units
- if appropriate in national circumstances, communicate their recommendations to all relevant stakeholders, including the relevant public managers, the finance ministry and the external auditor.

🌐 Examples from around the world	International Standards and Guidance	
United Kingdom: It is government policy that all departments should have professional finance directors and the finance director is responsible for leadership of financial responsibilities within the organisation. The finance director should maintain strong and effective policies to control and manage use of resources in the organisation's activities.	OECD Best Practices	3.2
	PEFA	PI – 19, 26
	GIFT Public Participation	XII

F	Supporting the role of the Supreme Audit Institution (SAI)

Supreme audit institutions (SAIs) should be instituted in a way that allows them to undertake independent, regular and high-quality audits. SAIs should be entrusted with providing assurance on the compliance of government expenditure with the applicable laws, regulations and rules; auditing the year-end financial report of the Government; and, increasingly, assessing the efficiency and effectiveness of public policies and programmes.

F.1 Core principles of Supreme Audit Institution (SAI) establishment and governance are laid down in the International Standards of SAIs (ISSAIs) as adopted by INTOSAI (the International Organisation of SAIs). These core principles cover auditing precepts, SAI independence as well as practical guidance for conduct of audit. SAIs should be instituted in a way that allows them to operate in compliance with the standards.

☞ **Suggested starting points** in considering such core issues are that SAIs should:

- be granted assured and stable financial and human resources, and unrestricted access to information in order to perform their audit mandate

- maintain documented, public procedures and codes to underpin their professional standards (e.g. ethics and audit manuals)

- engage with a variety of stakeholders (including parliament, media and civil society) and provide relevant, timely information on their work programme and findings

- ideally, elevate findings on cross-cutting issues to provide insight on efficiency, effectiveness, sustainability and integrity in public expenditure across government.

🌐 **Examples from around the world**

Brazil: Brazil's Supreme Audit Institution (the TCU) is constitutionally mandated to audit the performance and Accounts of the Federal Executive. The accounts are judged on elements of regularity and performance. The TCU also uses surveys, research and informational sessions with external stakeholders as a means of strengthening audit proceedings. TCU's guidance for auditors is based on international standards and linked to the multi-annual strategic plans of the institution.

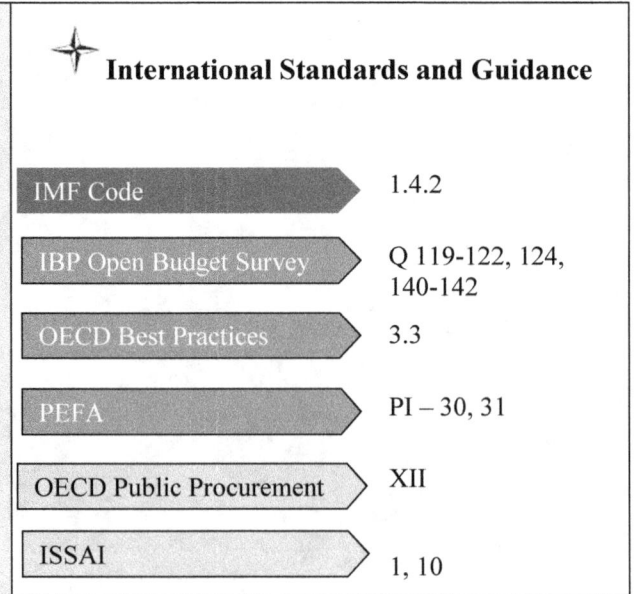

International Standards and Guidance	
IMF Code	1.4.2
IBP Open Budget Survey	Q 119-122, 124, 140-142
OECD Best Practices	3.3
PEFA	PI – 30, 31
OECD Public Procurement	XII
ISSAI	1, 10

F.2 **The external audit report** provides an independent and authoritative review of the **year-end reporting (see A.8)** of both budget execution and of financial statements by the SAI. This mainly shows whether the government's reporting is accurate and reliable, and indicates whether the government has complied with financial management laws and regulations. This report can also yield important messages for policy-makers, parliamentarians and the public regarding issues of corruption, fraud, mismanagement and wastefulness of resources.

☞ **Suggested starting points** for the external audit report are that it should:

- be conducted using generally accepted / ISSAI auditing practices
- be submitted to parliament as soon as practicable after the year-end reporting (**A.8**)
- ideally, include audit of reported performance information.

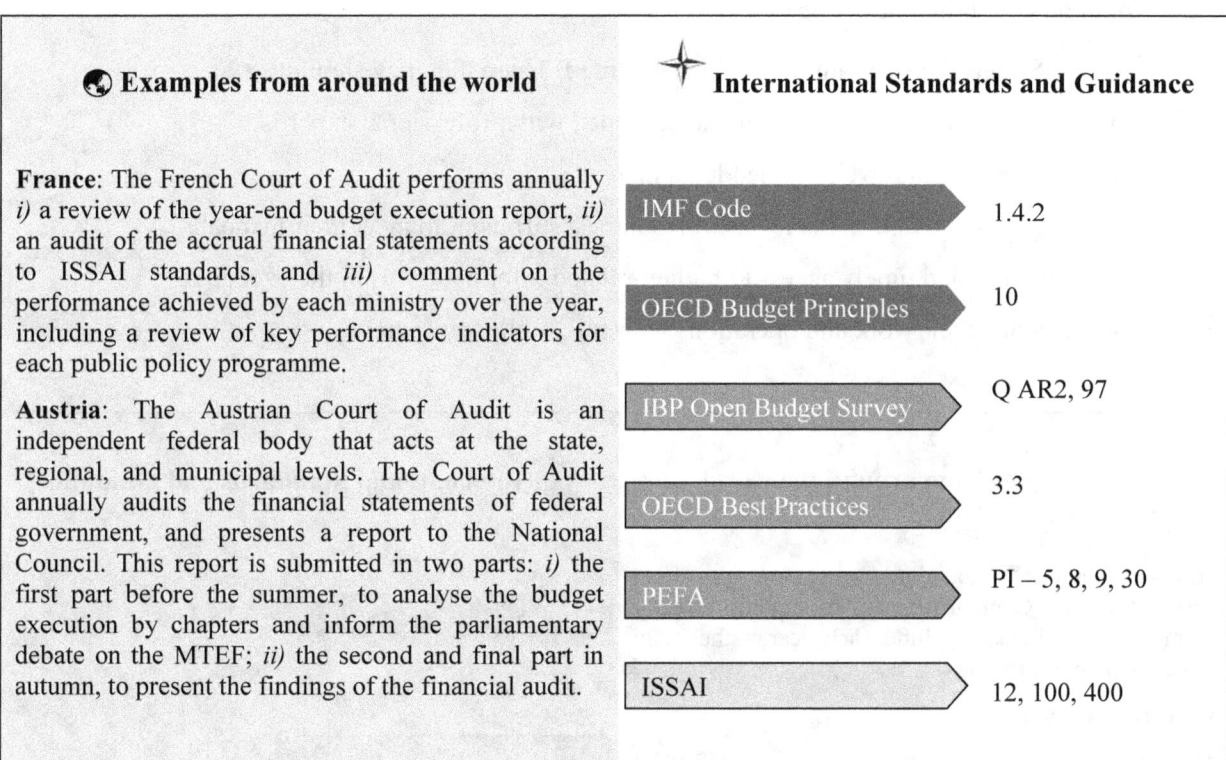

🌐 **Examples from around the world**

France: The French Court of Audit performs annually *i)* a review of the year-end budget execution report, *ii)* an audit of the accrual financial statements according to ISSAI standards, and *iii)* comment on the performance achieved by each ministry over the year, including a review of key performance indicators for each public policy programme.

Austria: The Austrian Court of Audit is an independent federal body that acts at the state, regional, and municipal levels. The Court of Audit annually audits the financial statements of federal government, and presents a report to the National Council. This report is submitted in two parts: *i)* the first part before the summer, to analyse the budget execution by chapters and inform the parliamentary debate on the MTEF; *ii)* the second and final part in autumn, to present the findings of the financial audit.

International Standards and Guidance

IMF Code	1.4.2
OECD Budget Principles	10
IBP Open Budget Survey	Q AR2, 97
OECD Best Practices	3.3
PEFA	PI – 5, 8, 9, 30
ISSAI	12, 100, 400

G	An effective role for Independent Fiscal Institutions (IFIs)

Many countries have established Independent Fiscal Institutions (independent parliamentary budget offices and fiscal councils) which can improve the objectivity of macroeconomic and budgetary forecasting, and enhance fiscal discipline through a 'watchdog' role in the national fiscal framework. IFIs can also promote greater fiscal transparency and accountability by raising the quality of national public debate on fiscal policy.

G.1 Design of an IFI must take account of country-specific circumstances, including constitutional roles and cultural traditions, so that the IFI can fit within the institutional budgetary "architecture" in a useful and impactful way, which underpins public confidence in the quality and professionalism of budgetary decision-making. While IFIs therefore vary in structure and function across countries, there are some common core principles to be observed.

▷ **Suggested starting points** in designing IFIs are that they should:

- be independent, non-partisan and equipped with professional expertise
- have a clear and well-defined legal mandate
- have assured and stable levels of resources, sufficient to meet their mandate
- have full and timely access to budget-related information from the executive
- conduct their work and operations with full public transparency.

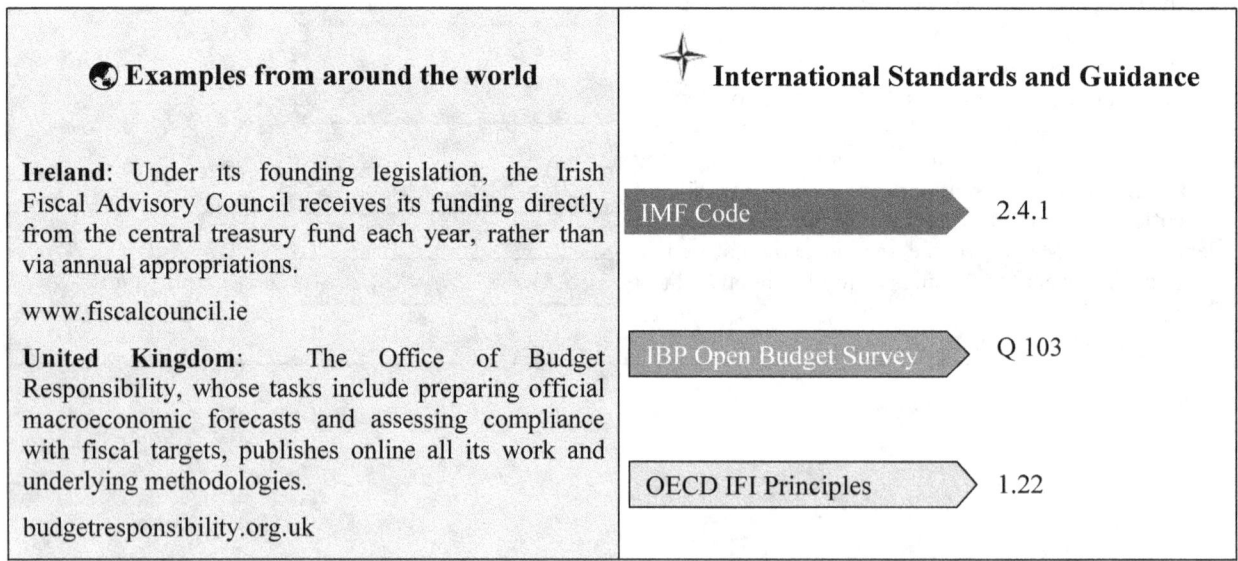

🌐 Examples from around the world	International Standards and Guidance
Ireland: Under its founding legislation, the Irish Fiscal Advisory Council receives its funding directly from the central treasury fund each year, rather than via annual appropriations. www.fiscalcouncil.ie **United Kingdom**: The Office of Budget Responsibility, whose tasks include preparing official macroeconomic forecasts and assessing compliance with fiscal targets, publishes online all its work and underlying methodologies. budgetresponsibility.org.uk	IMF Code — 2.4.1 IBP Open Budget Survey — Q 103 OECD IFI Principles — 1.22

G.2   Tasks and functions of IFIs should be selected to enhance the overall quality of budget-related decision-making and debate. The precise role of an IFI varies from country to country, and there is no single standard model for such an institution. There is, however, much international experience and guidance to draw upon when considering suitable roles for an IFI. It should also be noted that some countries have more than one institution with complementary roles – for example, a parliamentary budget office which provides budgetary analysis to the legislature (see **Section D.1** above) together with a fiscal council tasked with assessing government forecasts and monitoring fiscal rules.

☞ **Suggested starting points** in considering appropriate functions for IFIs include:

- assessing, endorsing, or producing official macroeconomic and/or fiscal forecasts
- analysing budgets and fiscal plans, and monitoring compliance with fiscal rules
- evaluating the mid- and long-term sustainability of public finances
- providing cost estimates for proposed policy measures.

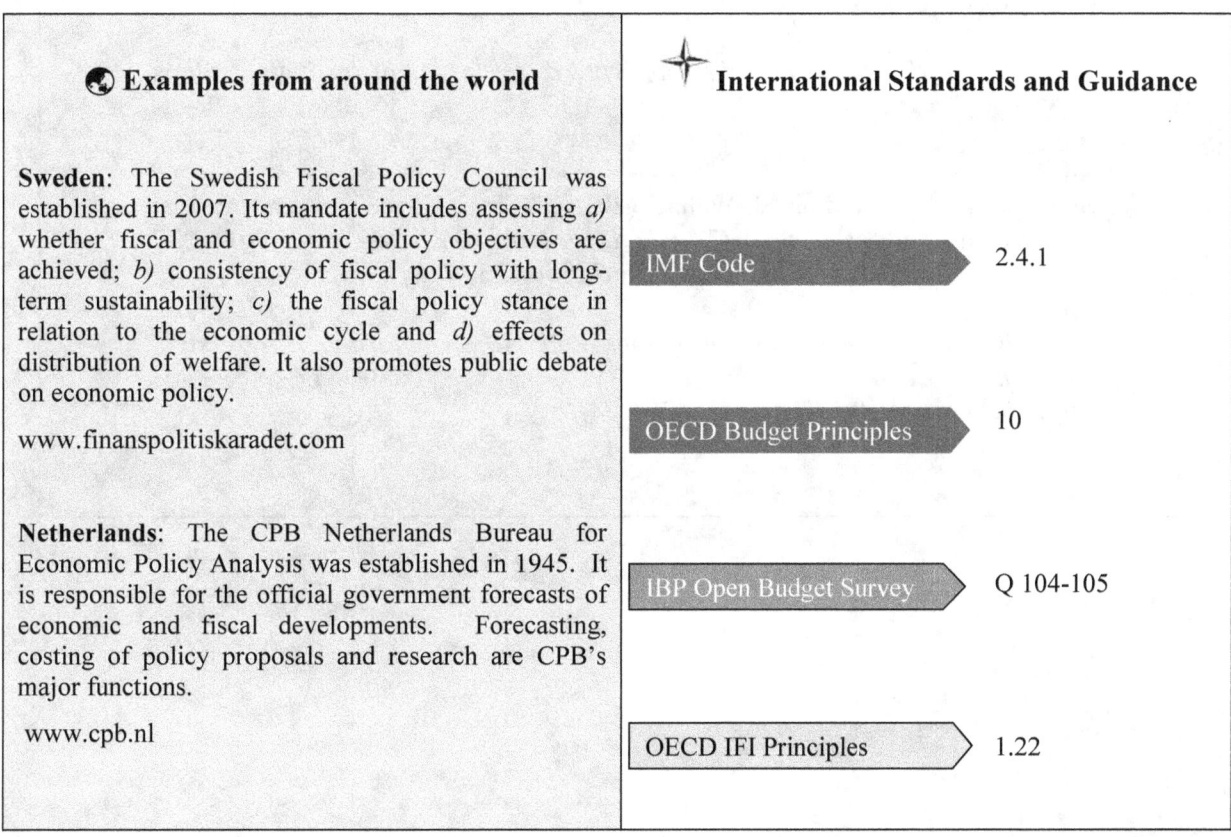

🌐 Examples from around the world	International Standards and Guidance	
Sweden: The Swedish Fiscal Policy Council was established in 2007. Its mandate includes assessing *a)* whether fiscal and economic policy objectives are achieved; *b)* consistency of fiscal policy with long-term sustainability; *c)* the fiscal policy stance in relation to the economic cycle and *d)* effects on distribution of welfare. It also promotes public debate on economic policy. www.finanspolitiskaradet.com	IMF Code	2.4.1
	OECD Budget Principles	10
Netherlands: The CPB Netherlands Bureau for Economic Policy Analysis was established in 1945. It is responsible for the official government forecasts of economic and fiscal developments. Forecasting, costing of policy proposals and research are CPB's major functions. www.cpb.nl	IBP Open Budget Survey	Q 104-105
	OECD IFI Principles	1.22

Further guidance

Hagemann, R. (2011), "How Can Fiscal Councils Strengthen Fiscal Performance?", *OECD Journal: Economic Studies*, Vol. 2011/1. http://dx.doi.org/10.1787/eco_studies-2011-5kg2d3gx4d5c

IMF (2015), *Tax Administration Diagnostic Assessment Tool (TADAT)*, http://www.tadat.org/

IMF (2013), *The Functions and Impact of Fiscal Councils,* International Monetary Fund, Washington D.C. www.imf.org/external/np/pp/eng/2013/071613.pdf

IMF (2014), *Strengthening Post-Crisis Fiscal Credibility: Fiscal Councils on the Rise, A New Dataset*, www.imf.org/external/pubs/ft/wp/2014/wp1458.pdf

Kopits, G. (2011), "Independent Fiscal Institutions: Developing Good Practices", *OECD Journal on Budgeting*, Vol. 11/3. http://dx.doi.org/10.1787/budget-11-5kg3pdgcpn42

OECD (2011), *Good Practices in Supporting Supreme Audit Institutions*, Paris, www.oecd.org/dac/effectiveness/Final%20SAI%20Good%20Practice%20Note.pdf

von Trapp, L., I. Lienert and J. Wehner (2016), "Principles for independent fiscal institutions and case studies", *OECD Journal on Budgeting*, Vol. 15/2. http://dx.doi.org/10.1787/budget-15-5jm2795tv625

OECD (2016), *Supreme Audit Institutions and Good Governance: Oversight, Insight and Foresight*, OECD Publishing, Paris. http://dx.doi.org/10.1787/9789264263871-en

 Openness and civic engagement

Citizens should have the right and all non-state actors, should have effective opportunities to participate directly in public debate and discussion over the design and implementation of fiscal policies.

- GIFT High Level Principles on Fiscal Transparency

Provide for an inclusive, participative and realistic debate on budgetary choices, by facilitating the engagement of parliaments, citizens and civil society organisations in a realistic debate about key priorities, trade-offs, opportunity costs and value for money

- OECD Recommendation on Budgetary Governance

The government provides citizens with an accessible summary of the implications of budget policies and an opportunity to participate in budget deliberations.

- IMF Code on Fiscal Transparency

	In this section
H	Making the budget information accessible to the public
I	Using open data to support budget transparency
J	Making the budget more inclusive and participative

H	Making the budget information accessible to the public

Budget documents and data can often be very dense, complex, and hard for ordinary citizens – or indeed for parliamentarians and budget practitioners – to understand and use. Making budget documents and information easy for people to access and understand, during all phases of the budget process, helps to ensure public understanding, thus increasing the quality of overall public discussion and parliamentary debate, and underpinning trust in government.

H.1 Presenting key budget information in a clear manner, that can be understood easily by the public and by civil-society stakeholders, goes to the heart of budget transparency. Without clear information about where money is going and for what purposes, it is more difficult for the government to generate support and understanding for its policy decisions or to be held accountable. Careful attention should therefore be paid to the presentation and communication of budget-related information.

▷ **Suggested starting points** in presenting budget information clearly include:

- presenting budget tables and 'headline' figures as simply and directly as possible, in a format that is consistent from year to year and from document to document
- including a high-level summary of all budget policy measures and their impacts
- putting abstract numbers into perspective with user-friendly graphics and charts.

Examples from around the world

United States: The Office of Management and Budget (OMB) provides Analytical Perspectives of budget which contains analyses that are designed to highlight specified subject areas or provide other significant presentations of budget data that place the budget in perspective. It also supplies Historical Tables which provide a wide range of data on Federal Government finances and Economic Assumptions from the 1970s.

International Standards and Guidance

IMF Code	2.3.3
OECD Budget Principles	4
IBP Open Budget Survey	Q GQ1d
OECD Best Practices	3.4
PEFA	PI - 9

H.2 Publishing a citizen's budget along with the actual public budget improves citizen's understanding of government policies and increases the transparency of policy-making. A citizen's budget is a simpler, less technical version of a government's budget specifically designed to present key information to the public, by summarising key content from the budget document in a user-friendly way. The essential components of a useful citizen's budget include expenditure and revenue totals, main budget policy initiatives and key macroeconomic forecasts. Ideally, citizen-friendly documents should be produced for all key publications linked to the budget cycle (e.g. year-end reports, audit reports, mid-term budget reports).

Suggested starting points regarding the development of a citizen's budget include:

- consulting citizens in advance, to design it around their needs and information gaps
- using clear, simple language and illustrations, to engage people of different ages, interests and levels of literacy
- using it to help citizens find fuller details within the main budget documentation
- producing it in a timely manner, with or soon after the main budget documentation
- communicating and disseminating it widely to reach its intended audience.

🌐 Examples from around the world	International Standards and Guidance	
Ghana: was one of the first African countries to publish a citizen's budget in 2006. Today, the ministry of finance runs a special Citizens' Budget website (http://myghanabudget.org/) and the 2016 Citizen's Budget was translated into seven local languages.	IMF Code	2.3.3
	OECD Budget Principles	4
Mexico: The Mexican Ministry of Finance publishes a citizen's budget annually since 2010. Since 2014, a citizen's version of the year-end report and the executive proposal are published as well. The citizen's budget is prepared in collaboration with CSOs.	IBP Open Budget Survey	Q 64-67
	PEFA	PI - 9

I	Using open data to support budget transparency

Making budget data publicly available in open digital form provides citizens and civil-society organisations with a valuable resource to analyse, evaluate and participate in public budgeting. Open budget data enables the public to understand and engage with the budgetary process and policy-making and to contribute new and innovative perspectives.

I.1 Open data should meet minimum standards of form and nature, which are of fundamental importance in determining who can use the data and in which ways. To ensure compatibility for a broad range of uses, **open data should allow users to compare, combine and follow the connections among different data sets.**

☞ **Suggested starting points** are that the open data should be:

- published in machine readable, preferably open-source formats on the internet

- disaggregated, editable, reusable, comparable and inter-operable

- bulk-downloadable to allow for use in research and analysis

- accompanied with information on data source, time of publication and licensing

- maintained over the long term (historical data) with appropriate version tracking.

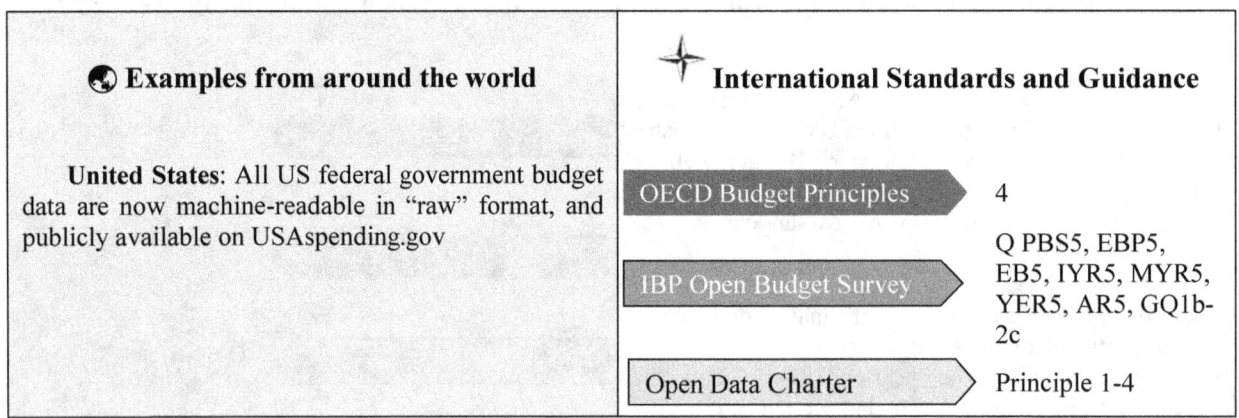

🌐 **Examples from around the world**

United States: All US federal government budget data are now machine-readable in "raw" format, and publicly available on USAspending.gov

✦ **International Standards and Guidance**

OECD Budget Principles	4
IBP Open Budget Survey	Q PBS5, EBP5, EB5, IYR5, MYR5, YER5, AR5, GQ1b-2c
Open Data Charter	Principle 1-4

I.2 Access to open budget data is essential if it is to meet its potential of contributing to broad public understanding and enriching the quality of analysis and debate on budget issues. Lowering access barriers depends on careful attention to how the data is presented. Ideally, all budget data should be "open by default" so that the data can be used in a routine manner for the purposes of scrutiny, accountability and public debate.

⌲ **Suggested starting points** regarding access to open budget data are that it should be:

- freely available without access fees or the need to register
- available on one integrated portal that allows for user-defined dynamic queries
- provided in a regular and timely manner to sustain public engagement
- linked to data-visualisation tools to help get the most value and use from the data.

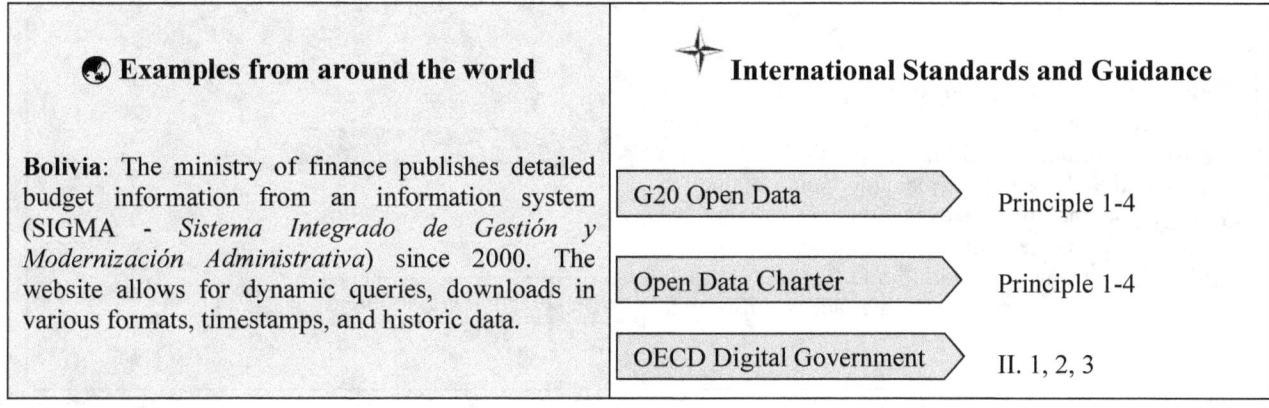

🌐 Examples from around the world	✢ International Standards and Guidance	
Bolivia: The ministry of finance publishes detailed budget information from an information system (SIGMA - *Sistema Integrado de Gestión y Modernización Administrativa*) since 2000. The website allows for dynamic queries, downloads in various formats, timestamps, and historic data.	G20 Open Data	Principle 1-4
	Open Data Charter	Principle 1-4
	OECD Digital Government	II. 1, 2, 3

I.3 Integrating open budget data portals with existing portals, and making them compliant with existing legislation and regulations, broadens the reach and the impact of the data.

☞ **Suggested starting points** are the open budget data portals should be:

- protected according to privacy and data protection laws
- published directly from the underlying financial management information system (FMIS), with a description of the underlying data available on the open data portal
- using common metadata and vocabularies, allowing international comparisons.

🌐 Examples from around the world	International Standards and Guidance
Brazil: The website of the ministry of finance is a centralised source of information. It provides extensive information and links to public finance sites such as the 'integrated planning and budgeting system', and the 'budget execution reports' that are published from the FMIS. A 'citizen information service', a 'transparency portal' and the 'get smart in public money' programme create accessibility and encourage public participation.	OECD Budget Principles — 4 OECD Digital Government — 10, 11

J	Making the budget more inclusive and participative

While proposing and implementing the budget are the legal duty of the executive, strengthening the involvement and participation of citizens and civil society can increase responsiveness, efficiency, impact and trust. Naturally, it is important that such approaches should be compatible with national legal frameworks and should complement, and not undermine, well-functioning processes of representative democracy. Heightened citizen engagement also reduces opportunities for corruption and strengthens the culture of open democracy.

J.1 Opportunities for participative approaches across the budget cycle and with different institutions should be developed, through introducing open, innovative and responsible approaches. As a general principle, participative approaches should aim to complement established legal and constitutional mandates, and so designed to enhance the effectiveness of policy-making and accountability at each stage.

⚑ **Suggested starting points** regarding opportunities for participative approaches are:

- timely consultative processes during the budget cycle should be considered, taking into account the knowledge, interests and capacities of citizens

- enhance parliamentary engagement and consultation with citizens during the phases of the policy and budget cycle where parliament is most actively involved

- Supreme Audit Institutions (SAIs) can benefit from the feedback of people and groups who receive public services, to gain insights into the quality of budget execution and the design of audit programmes.

🌐 **Examples from around the world**

Ireland: The National Economic Dialogue is a pre-budget consultative forum which brings together the various civil society and parliamentary stakeholders to discuss priorities for the October budget. The forum is held in June, after the government has determined (from its spring budget semester) the level of "fiscal space" available in the coming year, and before line ministries have submitted budget proposals. The Forum is moderated by an independent chairperson and all of its sessions are held in public.

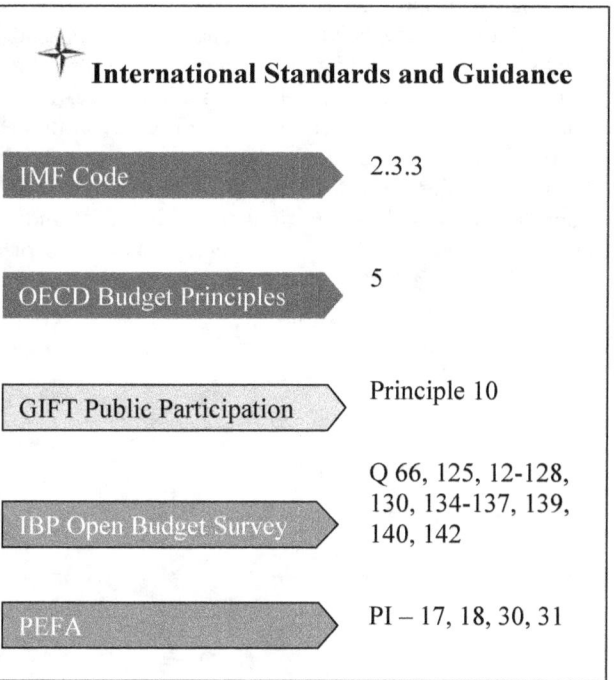

International Standards and Guidance

IMF Code	2.3.3
OECD Budget Principles	5
GIFT Public Participation	Principle 10
IBP Open Budget Survey	Q 66, 125, 12-128, 130, 134-137, 139, 140, 142
PEFA	PI – 17, 18, 30, 31

J.2 Realistic and informed public participation is necessary to ensure that the public can form an overview of budget design, results and impacts, and to set the basis for a productive and meaningful engagement with other stakeholders in the budget process.

☞ **Suggested starting points** to support realistic and informed participation are:

- information on budgetary constraints, policy costings, opportunity costs and policy trade-offs, as well as contributions to major policy goals and cross-sectoral issues
- effects on income and wellbeing classified by income groups and household types
- impacts on different groups in society, in particular the vulnerable or marginalised
- ideally, multi-dimensional impacts of policy options, including e.g. economic, social and environmental impacts, as well as effects on gender equality; noting that such impact assessments may also be provided through more general government reporting, rather than through budget-specific reports.

🌐 Examples from around the world	✦ International Standards and Guidance	
Korea: Six mechanisms are used that span the entire budget cycle. During the budget formulation stage, *1)* formalised open discussions for the public are held *2)* representatives from the Ministry of Finance hold meetings with local government officials and citizens *3)* a fiscal policy advisory council" reviews and finalises the budget, and *4)* an assembly expert hearing is conducted. During the implementation stage, *5)* a budget waste reporting centre" can be used by citizens to report any suspected misuse or waste of public funding. In the auditing stage, *6)* citizens have the opportunity to make suggestions to the board of audit and inspection on which public entity operations or expenditures to audit.	IMF Code	2.3.3
	OECD Budget Principles	5
	IBP Open Budget Survey	Q 36, 52, 94
	GIFT Public Participation	Principle 6
	G20 Open Data	Principle 5

J.3 Designing a participation process should aim to demonstrate its usefulness and relevance for budget policy-making, thus helping to sustain the approach across policy cycles and different administrations. It is helpful if the legal framework allows for, and supports, an orderly and transparent approach to public participation.

⚑ **Suggested starting points** regarding the design of a participation process include:

- publishing clear objectives, scope and process of public engagement in budgeting
- tailoring methods of engagement that are best suited to the various participants
- using a mix of mechanisms, proportionate to the nature of the issue concerned
- allowing enough time for the results from participation to impact on budget policy
- following up and giving citizens timely feedback about progress and results
- making sure that the most vulnerable parts of the population are included.

🌐 **Examples from around the world**

Philippines: established the Budget Partnership Agreement (BPA) as a mechanism for CSO engagement with national government agencies in drafting budget proposals. This instrument is only one of many introduced in the Philippines to make budgeting more participative. A public participation score of 67 in the 2015 Open Budget Survey acknowledges these efforts.

✦ **International Standards and Guidance**

| GIFT High Level Principles | 1, 2, 4, 6, 7, 8 |
| IBP Open Budget Survey | Q 126, 129, 131-133, 138, 141 |

Further guidance

IBP (2012), *The power of making it simple*, www.internationalbudget.org/publications/the-power-of-making-it-simple-a-government-guide-to-developing-citizens-budgets/

IBP (2017), Web resource on citizen's budgets, www.internationalbudget.org/opening-budgets/citizens-budgets/

Partners of the Americas (2006), Involving Citizens in Public Budgets – Mechanisms for Transparent and Participatory Budgeting, Partners of the Americas, Washington D. C., www.internationalbudget.org/publications/involving-citizens-in-public-budgets-mechanisms-for-transparent-and-participatory-budgeting/

Petrie, M. and Shields, J. (2010): "Producing a Citizens' Guide to the Budget: Why, What and How?" in *OECD Journal on Budgeting*, Vol. 10/2. http://dx.doi.org/10.1787/budget-10-5km7gkwg2pjh

Dener, C. and Min, S. Y. (2013): *Financial Management Information Systems and Open Budget Data*, The World Bank, Washington D. C., www-wds.worldbank.org/external/default/WDSContentServer/WDSP/IB/2013/09/26/000356161_20130926123854/Rendered/PDF/813320PUB0Fina00Box374313B00PUBLIC0.pdf

G20 (2015), *Introductory note to the G20 anti-corruption open data principles*, http://www.g20.utoronto.ca/2015/G20-Anti-Corruption-Open-Data-Principles.pdf

Gray, J. (2015), *Open Budget Data - mapping the landscape*, Global Initiative for Fiscal Transparency (GIFT), www.fiscaltransparency.net/resourcesfiles/files/20150902128.pdf

OECD (forthcoming), *Digital Government Toolkit*

OECD (2014), *Recommendation of the Council on Digital Government Strategies*, OECD Publishing, Paris, www.oecd.org/gov/digital-government/Recommendation-digital-government-strategies.pdf

Fölscher, A. (2007), "A Primer on Effective Participation" in Shah, A. (ed.), Participatory Budgeting, The World Bank, Washington D. C., p. 243-255, http://siteresources.worldbank.org/PSGLP/Resources/ParticipatoryBudgeting.pdf

Marchessault, L. (2015), Public Participation and the Budget Cycle: Lessons from Country Examples, Global Initiative for Fiscal Transparency (GIFT), www.fiscaltransparency.net/resourcesfiles/files/20151116137.pdf

OECD (2015), *Policy Shaping and Policy Making: The Governance of Inclusive Growth*, OECD Publishing, Paris, www.oecd.org/governance/ministerial/the-governance-of-inclusive-growth.pdf

Open Contracting Partnership (2014), *Open Contracting Data Standard*.

 Promoting integrity with the private sector

"The Government sector should be clearly defined and identified for the purposes of reporting, transparency, and accountability, and government financial relationships with the private sector should be disclosed, conducted in an open manner, and follow clear rules and procedures."

- GIFT High Level Principle 6

"Ensure an adequate degree of transparency of the public procurement system in all stages of the procurement cycle [...] and support integration of public procurement into overall public finance management, budgeting and services delivery processes"

- OECD Recommendation on Public Procurement 2015

"There is emerging evidence that open contracting can save governments money and time, prevent corruption and fraud, create a better business environment, boost small businesses, and help deliver better goods and services to citizens."

- Open Contracting Partnership (OCP) Strategy 2015 l 2018

"We recognise that a public understanding of government revenues and expenditure over time could help public debate and inform choice of appropriate and realistic options for sustainable development."

- 4th EITI-Principle

	In this section
K	Opening up public contracting and procurement
L	Accounting for revenues and expenditures in resource endowments
M	Managing infrastructure investment for integrity, value for money and transparency

K	Opening up public contracting and procurement
	Making public contracting and procurement open creates transparency, enables participation, increases access to government contracts, and improves value for money. It involves the entire contracting cycle from planning to closing of a contract. The kind and amount of information disclosed needs to be comprehensive, subject to data security and privacy regulations.

K.1 Making the entire public procurement cycle open allows a fair and equitable treatment for potential suppliers. By increasing competition and enabling participation, it contributes to getting better value for money. Increased transparency reduces the risk of collusion and corruption.

☞ **Suggested starting points** are that the principle of openness should apply to:

- the public procurement system (institutional frameworks, regulations, procedures)
- open and competitive tender
- the full set of bidding documents, evaluation reports, and contract documents
- the performance of the public procurement system (monitoring results, data)
- associated risks, assets, and liabilities of the government related to the contract
- integration of procurement processes with public financial management.

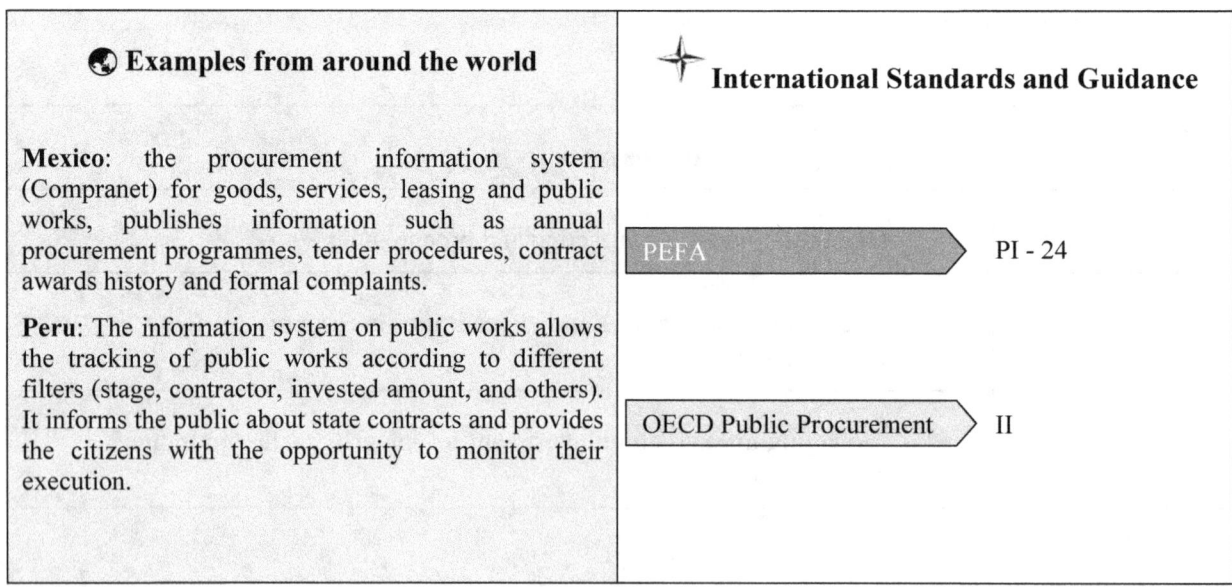

🌐 **Examples from around the world**

Mexico: the procurement information system (Compranet) for goods, services, leasing and public works, publishes information such as annual procurement programmes, tender procedures, contract awards history and formal complaints.

Peru: The information system on public works allows the tracking of public works according to different filters (stage, contractor, invested amount, and others). It informs the public about state contracts and provides the citizens with the opportunity to monitor their execution.

International Standards and Guidance

PEFA → PI - 24

OECD Public Procurement → II

K.2 Using e-procurement tools increases accessibility to, and fairness of government contracting. The digital approach increases efficiency and effectiveness of public procurement through standardisation of the process and more competition. It is helpful to have legislation, regulation and policy in place that allow or mandate the use of electronic methods and instruments for public procurement.

Suggested starting points regarding effective e-procurement solutions include:

- consistent coverage of the public procurement cycle across all levels of government
- a user-friendly approach, with tools that are easy to understand and use
- systems that ensure privacy, security of data and authentication, and fair treatment
- integration with existing systems such as financial management information system
- capacity development for users (government agencies and bidders/suppliers)
- clear communication to promote awareness and acceptance among users.

Examples from around the world

Korea: The fully integrated, end-to-end e-procurement system called KONEPS is mandatory for all public organisations. It includes a Fingerprint Recognition e-Bidding system to mitigate the risk of illegal practices. The system reduced transaction costs and increased participation in public tenders.

Ukraine: the e-procurement system ProZorro was launched in 2015. It has been developed by a public private partnership based on the Open Contracting Data Standard. It has been estimated to have saved USD 1.5 million of public funds in the first three month of piloting.

International Standards and Guidance

OECD Public Procurement — I, II, IV

K.3 Fostering realistic and effective stakeholder participation in the public procurement system enables more dialogue and control and thereby decreases risk. A participative approach also helps to reduce opportunities for fraud and corruption. Some general approaches to promoting a participative approach in budget-related policy-making, including a supportive legal and regulatory framework, are set out in section J of this Toolkit

⚑ **Suggested starting points** regarding participative approaches in this area include:

- a consultative process when formulating changes to the public procurement system (e.g. amending laws and regulations)
- regular dialogues with suppliers and business operations to present public procurement objectives and to ensure a correct understanding of markets
- a transparent and independent mechanism for resolving substantive disputes
- consider drawing on civil society mechanisms for monitoring the integrity of public procurement.

🌐 Examples from around the world	International Standards and Guidance	
United Kingdom: Debriefing discussions are held within a maximum of 15 days after the contract award. The sessions are chaired by senior procurement personnel who have been involved in the procurement. The debriefing covers: an open explanation of the procurement selection and evaluation process; the strengths and weaknesses of the supplier's bid; and a description of the supplier's views on the process. A note of the meeting is made for the record.	OECD Budget Principles	5
	PEFA	PI - 24
	OECD Public Procurement	II, VI

L	Accounting for revenues and expenditures in resource endowments

Transparency in the extractive sector is of special relevance, because in resource-rich countries this sector can generate a significant share of all public revenues. At the same time the technical complexity and involvement of only a limited number of companies and government agencies poses a high integrity risk. Related issues of sustainability and inter-generational equity can also benefit from increased transparency.

L.1 Fully reflecting public extractive sector revenues in budget-related documents contributes to full transparency, public participation and monitoring. Given the particular vulnerabilities to corruption in the extractive sector, there is a particular onus for the principles of openness and budget transparency to be applied with rigour.

☞ **Suggested starting points** are that the budget-related documents should detail clearly:

- resource revenues such as profit taxes, royalties, dividends, fees, and concessions
- government receipts of company resource revenue payments (see also **L.3**)
- finances and operations of any Natural Resources Funds and any public corporations engaged in resource extraction or sale
- the non-resource fiscal balance as well as the overall balance
- estimates and forecasts on resource asset worth and resource revenue development
- risks associated with resource revenues and the volatility of the sector.

🌐 **Examples from around the world**

Norway complies with the EITI standard since 2011. In addition to publishing an annual EITI-report, it makes the EITI data available on the government data transparency portal. Also, the Norwegian central bank (Norges Bank) annually and quarterly publishes reports providing information about the fund used to administrate the resource revenues. It includes information about transfers to and from the budget, market trends, returns on investments and income, trends regarding risk exposure, and administrative costs.

✦ **International Standards and Guidance**

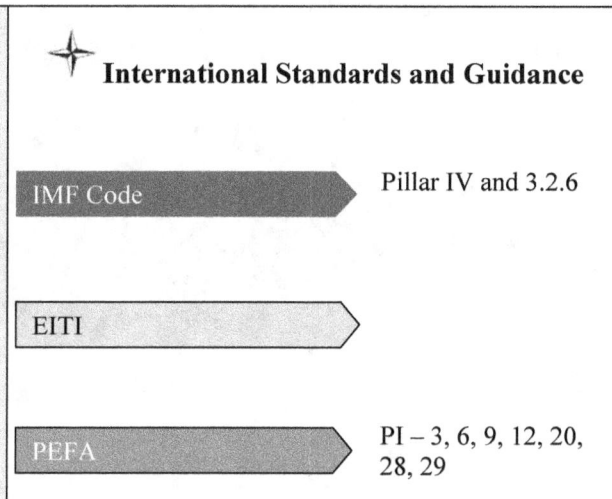

IMF Code — Pillar IV and 3.2.6

EITI

PEFA — PI – 3, 6, 9, 12, 20, 28, 29

L.2 Reporting how the money is used helps in the monitoring of financial flows thus making mismanagement and corruption easier to detect. This reporting should take place in the context of the regular budget-related documentation throughout the year.

🏳 **Suggested starting points** are that details should be provided on:

- how resource revenues are managed (on- or off-budget)
- resource revenue-sharing and/or expenditures for special resource-related programmes or sub-national government
- costs of 'quasi-fiscal activities' (e.g. large public infrastructure developments) conducted by state-owned resource companies
- the balance, flows, development and investment policies and operations of special designated funds, where these are used to manage resource revenues.

🌐 Examples from around the world	✛ International Standards and Guidance
Colombia: *MapaRegalías* is an online information system that uses visualisation to make it possible to trace the use of royalties from resource extraction. It gives citizens the opportunity to be informed about the revenue and how it is allocated between different levels of governments and institutions. Citizens can use the tool to monitor the progress of investment projects financed by royalties.	IMF Code → Pillar 4 EITI → PEFA → PI – 6, 19, 20

L.3 Complying with specialised international standards for resource endowments contributes to budget transparency with respect to resource revenues and expenditures and increases international credibility and trust.

🏁 **Suggested starting points** for international compliance include transparency about:

- the fiscal regime governing the extractive sector
- the level and nature of state participation in the extractive sector
- state-owned company production entitlement
- social and economic spending, to allow stakeholders to assess whether the extractive sector is leading to desirable social and economic impacts and outcomes
- published verification of government receipts of company resource revenue payments against reported company payments to government.

✣ International Standards and Guidance	
IMF Code	Pillar 4
EITI	2.7

M	Managing infrastructure investment for integrity, value for money and transparency
	Due to their large scale, technical complexity and large number of stakeholders, infrastructure projects are vulnerable to corruption, collusion and mismanagement. In order to minimise fiscal risks and to ensure the integrity of the investment process, infrastructure needs to be managed in a transparent and effective manner, ensuring integrity, promoting transparent delivery choices and disclosing relevant data to the public.

M.1 Map corruption entry points at each stage of the project procurement to facilitate a strategic and thought-through approach to managing the corruption, waste and rent-seeking risks.

Suggested starting points in guarding against corruption in this area are:

- selection of projects clearly based on identified needs and the public interest
- estimations of costs and benefits that are credible and evidence-based
- fair, effective and non-discriminatory standards to qualify for tendering bids
- mechanisms to underpin accountability and value for money in evaluation of bids
- audit checks of the project at various stages, e.g. by the supreme audit institution
- post-project evaluation to assess realisation of expected benefits.

Examples from around the world	International Standards and Guidance
United Kingdom: The "Gateway" process of the UK examines infrastructure projects at five critical stages (gateways) of their lifecycle. Each gateway needs to be cleared before the project can proceed to the next stage. The gateway reviews focuses on *1)* strategic assessment, *2)* business justification, *3)* delivery strategy, *4)* investment decision, *5)* readiness for service, and *6)* operations review and benefit realisation. This process helps to assess the progress and success as well as potential risks of the project.	IMF Code — 2.1.4 OECD Budget Principles — 3 PEFA — PI – 11, 12, 24, 30

M.2 Infrastructure assets must be affordable and represent value for money. Making sure that the asset delivers more benefits than costs provides some evidence of transparent and efficient delivery choices. For all infrastructure projects this also entails ensuring that there is an on-going competitive market, thereby facilitating competitive bidding for the contract. When comparing various forms of infrastructure delivery (e.g. private finance/concessions versus traditional public works) a set of principles and methodologies should ensure that the most cost-effective option is chosen. The project approval body (whether central budget authority, line ministry or agency) must make sure that users are willing and able to pay and/or that the medium term budget envelope has sufficient fiscal space to finance the asset.

☞ **Suggested starting points** to ensure value for money in this area include:

- establishing clear, objective standards and methods for comparing various alternative delivery/financing options – e.g. a 'public sector comparator'

- centralised professional scrutiny (e.g. within the Ministry of Finance) of all projects with respect to affordability and value for money

- a stable competitive market for infrastructure assets with competitive bidding and effective procurement (see section **K**)

- Cost-Benefit Analysis (CBA) of all infrastructure projects on a sound, uniform basis, identifying all prospective economic, social and environmental impacts, and consulting the affected public.

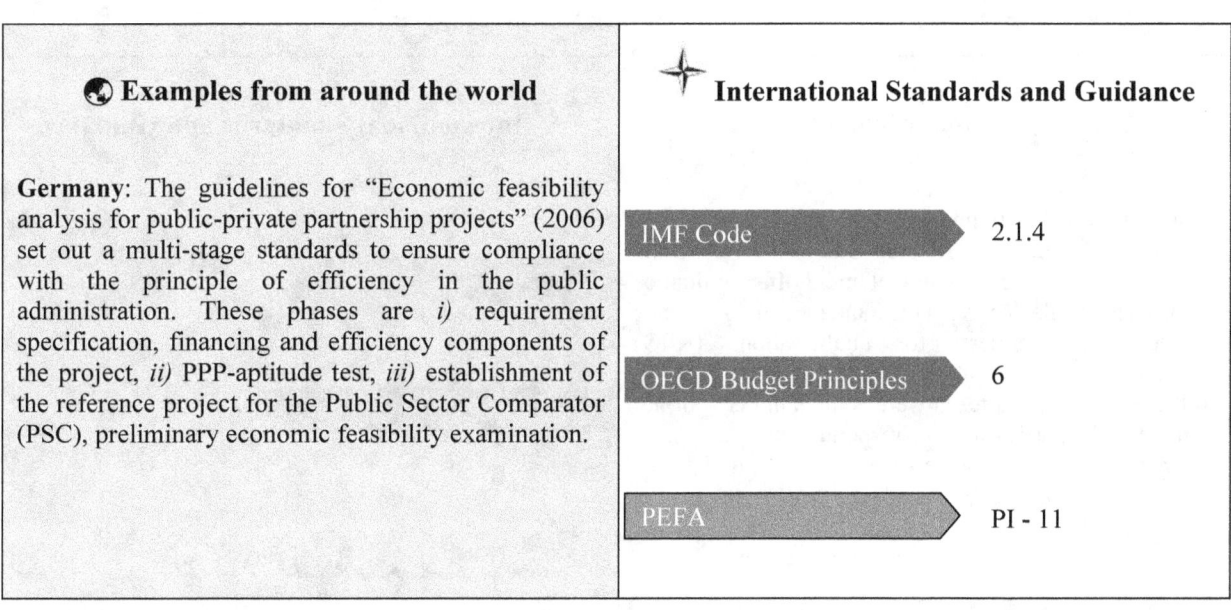

🌐 Examples from around the world	✛ International Standards and Guidance
Germany: The guidelines for "Economic feasibility analysis for public-private partnership projects" (2006) set out a multi-stage standards to ensure compliance with the principle of efficiency in the public administration. These phases are *i)* requirement specification, financing and efficiency components of the project, *ii)* PPP-aptitude test, *iii)* establishment of the reference project for the Public Sector Comparator (PSC), preliminary economic feasibility examination.	IMF Code — 2.1.4 OECD Budget Principles — 6 PEFA — PI - 11

M.3. The proactive disclosure of relevant data including key budget data to the public in a timely and accessible fashion, enhances transparency, competition, confidence and value for money in the procurement and delivery of infrastructure projects.

⚑ **Suggested starting points** regarding proactive disclosure in this area, subject to clear national rules regarding disclosure of commercially-sensitive or otherwise confidential data, include:

- basic project information, contract dates and deadlines, links to all contract documents, and contact details of relevant parties
- the project appraisal and independent review of appraisal
- details on the assessed total and year-by-year project costs, listing of risks with information on who bears the risk, evaluation of procurement options, and financial information
- potential government support in the form of guarantees, grants, service payments, land leases, asset transfers, and revenue shares
- tariffs and pricing, events of default and termination payments, and renegotiations
- performance information, project monitoring details and details on disposable assets
- all payments, revenues, liabilities, contingent liabilities, and commitments are clearly incorporated in the budget documentation and the year-end reporting (**A.8**).

🌍 Examples from around the world	✢ International Standards and Guidance
British Columbia (Canada): With the 2012 updated policy for Procurement Related Disclosure for Public Private Partnerships, British Columbia offers guidance on proactive disclosure. This guidance recommends for example, requests for qualifications (RFQ) documents through a project website or through a link to the B.C. bid website, as well as the number (but not names) of parties who respond to the RFQ. Furthermore the disclosure of names and numbers of parties that are short-listed at RFQ stage are recommended, as well as the disclosure of the preferred proponent when evaluation is advanced.	IMF Code ▶ 2.1.4 OECD Budget Principles ▶ 6 PEFA ▶ PI – 5, 6, 8, 9, 11, 12, 29

Further guidance

G20 (2015), *G20 Principles for Promoting Integrity in Public Procurement*, www.seffaflik.org/wp-content/uploads/2015/02/G20-PRINCIPLES-FOR-PROMOTING-INTEGRITY-IN-PUBLIC-PROCUREMENT.pdf

IMF (2007), *Guide on Resource Revenue Transparency*, International Monetary Fund, Washington D. C., www.imf.org/external/np/pp/2007/eng/101907g.pdf

IMF (2017), Public Investment Management Assessment website, www.imf.org/external/np/fad/publicinvestment/

IPSASB, *International Public Sector Accounting Standards 32* (Service Concession Arrangements)

OCP (2015), *2015 l 2018 Strategy*, Open Contracting Partnership (OCP), www.open-contracting.org/resources/strategy-2015-2018/

OCP (2013), *Open Contracting – A guide for practitioners by practitioners*, Open Contracting Partnership (OCP), www.unpcdc.org/media/416641/open_contracting_a_guide_for_practitioners_by_practitioners-v2.pdf

OECD (2015) High-Level Principles for Integrity, Transparency and Effective Control of Major Events and Related Large Infrastructure, OECD Publishing, Paris, www.oecd.org/gov/ethics/High-Level_Principles_Integrity_Transparency_Control_Events_Infrastructures.pdf

OECD (2016), *Integrity Framework for Public Investment*, OECD Publishing, Paris.
http://dx.doi.org/10.1787/9789264251762-en

OECD (2015), Towards a Framework for the Governance of Infrastructure, Paris, www.oecd.org/gov/budgeting/Towards-a-Framework-for-the-Governance-of-Infrastructure.pdf

OECD (2012), *Recommendation of the Council for the Public Governance of Public-Private Partnership*, OECD Publishing, Paris, www.oecd.org/governance/budgeting/PPP-Recommendation.pdf

OECD (2010), *Methodology for Assessing Procurement Systems (MAPS)*, Paris, www.oecd.org/dac/effectiveness/45181522.pdf

World Bank (2007), *Corruption and Technology in Public Procurement*, The World Bank, Washington D. C.,
http://documents.worldbank.org/curated/en/2007/04/10449733/corruption-technology-public-procurement

World Bank (2011), *e-Procurement Reference Guide*, The World Bank, Washington D. C., http://siteresources.worldbank.org/INFORMATIONANDCOMMUNICATIONANDTECHNOLOGIES/Resources/2011_WorldBankICT_eProcurement_Reference_Guide.docx

World Bank Public Investment Management (2017), website, http://web.worldbank.org/WBSITE/EXTERNAL/TOPICS/EXTPUBLICSECTORANDGOVERNANCE/0,,contentMDK:23136527~pagePK:148956~piPK:216618~theSitePK:286305,00.html

World Bank Group (2015), A Framework for Disclosure in Public-Private Partnership Projects, http://pubdocs.worldbank.org/en/773541448296707678/Disclosure-in-PPPs-Framework.pdf

Construction Sector Transparency Initiative (CoST), www.constructiontransparency.org

Annex: Transparency throughout the budget cycle

	Government	Parliament	Independent Oversight	Civil Society	Private Sector
Entire cycle	B.1-2 Including the right financial information in budget-related documents	C.1 Parliamentary committees D.1-2 Supporting parliamentary capacity	G.1 IFI engagement in the budget process	H.1 Presenting key budget information in a clear manner I. Using open data to support budget transparency J. Making the budget more inclusive and participative	L.3 Complying with the Extractive Industries Transparency Initiative (EITI) standard M. Managing infrastructure investment for integrity, value for money and transparency
Budget Formulation	A.1 The pre-budget statement A.2 The budget proposal	C.2 Ex-ante parliamentary engagement			L.1 Reflecting public extractive sector revenues in the budget

ANNEX: TRANSPARENCY THROUGHOUT THE BUDGET CYCLE

		C.3 Parliamentary approval of the budget		H.2 Publishing a citizen's budget	K. Opening up public contracting and procurement
Budget Approval	A.3 The approved budget				
Budget Execution	A.4 The supplementary budget		E. Management and internal control of public money		
	A.5 Pre-execution budget profiles				
	A.6 In-year budget execution reports				
	A.7 The mid-year implementation report				
Budget Review	A.8 Year-end reporting	C.4 Parliamentary scrutiny of budget execution and outturn	F. Supporting the role of the Supreme Audit Institution (SAI)		L.2 Reporting how the money is used
	A.9 The long-term report				
	A.10 Reporting on fiscal risk				

ORGANISATION FOR ECONOMIC CO-OPERATION AND DEVELOPMENT

The OECD is a unique forum where governments work together to address the economic, social and environmental challenges of globalisation. The OECD is also at the forefront of efforts to understand and to help governments respond to new developments and concerns, such as corporate governance, the information economy and the challenges of an ageing population. The Organisation provides a setting where governments can compare policy experiences, seek answers to common problems, identify good practice and work to co-ordinate domestic and international policies.

The OECD member countries are: Australia, Austria, Belgium, Canada, Chile, the Czech Republic, Denmark, Estonia, Finland, France, Germany, Greece, Hungary, Iceland, Ireland, Israel, Italy, Japan, Korea, Latvia, Luxembourg, Mexico, the Netherlands, New Zealand, Norway, Poland, Portugal, the Slovak Republic, Slovenia, Spain, Sweden, Switzerland, Turkey, the United Kingdom and the United States. The European Union takes part in the work of the OECD.

OECD Publishing disseminates widely the results of the Organisation's statistics gathering and research on economic, social and environmental issues, as well as the conventions, guidelines and standards agreed by its members.

www.ingramcontent.com/pod-product-compliance
Lightning Source LLC
Chambersburg PA
CBHW082344220526
45470CB00008B/2635